Diyar

# The Case for Humanity
## An Extraordinary Session

*Yasmine Maria Sherif*

*First Edition*

---

## The Case for Humanity
*An Extraordinary Session*

*Yasmine Maria Sherif*

*Copy right © 2014 Diyar Publisher*

*Art direction : Diyar Publisher*
*Designer : Engred Anwar Al-Khoury*
*Printing press: Latin Patriarchate*

---

---

*w w w . d i y a r . p s*

*"Somewhere, something incredible*
*is waiting to be known."*


*Carl Sagan*

*In memory of my beloved mother:*

*You saw the light*

*and kindled the flame.*

# Contents

Foreword ................................................................ 6

Introduction: *Adoption of a New Agenda* ..................... 8

1.    Vision and Mission: Making the Connection ................16

2. Leadership and Power: *Empowering Others* ................. 34

3. Values and Justice: *Appealing to the Essence* .............. 44

4. Courage and Conviction: *Dare Something Worthy* ......... 61

5. Intelligence and Knowledge:

   *Understanding the Immeasurable* ............................... 75

6. Hope and Belief: *Kindling the Light* .......................... 90

7. Freedom and Creativity: *Telling the Story* .................. 104

8. Individuals and Growth: *Remaking Ourselves* .............. 115

9. Humanity and Service: *A Spiritual Renaissance* ........... 123

Afterword: *Taking the Step* ...................................... 130

Acknowledgements .................................................. 137

Endnotes .............................................................. 141

# *FOREWORD*

Humanity is the most essential capacity we possess. It manifests in our daily lives, in our institutions, and on the political arena. Humanity means using our minds and hearts for the betterment of the human family in all situations of life. But humanity is not a stand-alone trait. It entails so many aspects of a person's hopes and relationship to others. It means justice, freedom and peace. It requires speaking truth to power. At the same time, humanity demands humility. It takes a lot of courage to uphold those standards of achievement, and admit when one fails without tiring to try again. It is never too late.

Where there is a will, there is a way. With that comes a willingness to self-examination and dialogue. It thrives on our yearning to find solutions that respond to the rights and duties in international law, our shared universal values. This requires moral integrity and inner strength. For it is only in showing solidarity with the downtrodden and the oppressed in the face of massive power that our humanity attains its full strength.

This book sheds light on the quest for humanity. Through a unique constellation by which over one hundred voices, well-known and unknown, debate in an imaginary setting of the United Nations Security Council, *The Case for Humanity* unfolds the factors that make up our humanity. This innovative debate is a positive and inspirational piece of work that gently and poignantly touches our hearts and minds. It does not judge, nor condemn. It simply opens the doorway to a deeper understanding, which is often bypassed or obscured in daily life. It is, therefore, a book that comes at the time when we most need it.

I have known Yasmine Sherif for over fifteen years, and have eagerly been awaiting her book *The Case for Humanity* all those years. When we first met at the United Nations, she shared with me a piece that she had authored on the subject of humanity. She was passionate and committed to search for its pearl beneath the surface. She was driven. I sensed that her early piece on humanity would evolve into something of significant importance one day.

In the years that followed, we continued our discussions in New York, Dili, Geneva and Jerusalem. She kept prodding and examining humanity through her work at the United Nations and in her personal reflections. And so, I came to follow the development of her book throughout these years. At the onset of the 21st century, I am delighted that *The Case for Humanity* is finally released. May it guide and inspire our generation, and all those yet to come.

*José Ramos-Horta*
*Nobel Peace Prize Laureate (1996)*
*Dili, 16 May 2015*

# *Introduction:*
# *Adoption of a New Agenda*

" *Learn how to see. Realize that everything connects to everything else.* "

*Leonardo da Vinci*

There is a fork in the road before us. Our systems, leaders and individual sense of meaning are at stake. We have to choose between *realpolitik* and ethical politics; between rigid structures to control, and creative spaces to serve; between separation and integration; and between desperation and inspiration. One track threatens to mire us in stagnation, while the other carries a promise of progress for each person, and the human family.

We have choices to make. Do we choose the 'will to power' or the 'will to humanity,' or, perhaps, a new configuration of both: *the power of humanity?*

As I write, over ten million people have fled their homes in war ravaged Syria, of whom hundreds of thousands seek refuge in Europe; while children, even whole families, perished in Gaza in the summer of 2014; the Central African Republic and South Sudan have again descended into ethnic violence; and Iraq has turned into a protracted battlefield. We look at such horrors, and ask: where is our humanity?

It is a cry born from our recent past: from the horrors of the Holocaust and the Gulag to the calamity of the Vietnam War, from ethnic cleansing in Bosnia-Herzegovina and genocide in Rwanda. It is a response to the many brutal tragedies resulting from man's inhumanity to man. It is a call that will not cease, a cry that will not be silenced – until we find our humanity.

I believe that the 'will to humanity' is larger than life itself. At its best, it freely imbues our very being, offering itself to alleviate suffering and to create beauty in the world. At its worst, it is perverted and overtaken by the raw 'will to power': something that the insightful German philosopher Nietzsche defined as humanity's predominant driving force.

The 'will to humanity' differs profoundly from the 'will to power.' Seated in the soul, it is sensitive, refined and authentic. It yearns to be discovered – and can be found through a journey within. It simultaneously defines the seven billion people dwelling on earth, as well as the light dwelling in each of those seven billion souls. Making the connection between the two is the ultimate goal to which we, the human species, can aspire.

Failing to make this connection has brought us where we are today. By acknowledging this disconnect I do not mean to stir negative reactions, but rather to fortify hope and inspire positive action. Universal values lie at the heart of our humanity, and their realization hinges on action. The core of these values is nondiscrimination: the belief that neither rights nor duties should discriminate between people or nations, but should rather unify us through universal standards of achievement. They represent our unrealized potential, the essence of our being: the power of humanity.

We can no longer afford to shun the journey to find that power. We have promises to keep:

"

*In this we shall not fail. An inner voice tells us that, animated by a broad and sincere feeling for humanity, we can lift up our hearts and bring to bear on the problems of peace, the spirit of cooperation, the tenacity of purpose, the self-sacrifice, and the technical effort, which, when applied to the dramatic problems of war, led to the splendid triumph of the de-mocracies that has enabled us to meet here today.* 🙦🙦[1]

These were the words of Dr. Zuleta Angel of Colombia, as he called to order the first United Nations General Assembly on 10 January 1946 in London. His words were born out of an era of unspeakable suffering and destruction that had torn open the hearts of peoples and nations alike. The culprit, the 'will to power' in its most ugly form, wrought those horrors of inhumanity and darkened the lives of tens of millions across the globe.

In making a commitment to 'never again' the international community, through the United Nations, pledged to protect the rights and freedoms of all human beings above geo-political, economic, national, sectarian and personal interests. The creation of the United Nations, and the proclamation of the Charter and the Universal Declaration of Human Rights, formed the nucleus of a collective effort to heal the world - just as light enters a wound, to paraphrase the Persian poet and Sufi mystic, Jalaluddin Rumi.

Generations later, we ask in frustration whether we are on the right path. "Only on paper has humanity yet achieved glory, beauty, truth, knowledge, virtue and abiding love,"[2] said the Irish playwright George Bernard Shaw. While some progress has been made, the past seventy years have also been amongst the more gruesome periods in the history of humankind. In both peace and war, violations of international law intended to protect people rapidly mount unchecked above our stack of conventions and global commitments.

The gulf between the law and reality is wide. In the dark abyss, billions of human beings still plead for humanity.

The great Chinese philosopher Confucius said: "Where words lose their meaning, people lose their liberty."[3] In today's world, subjective interests often overtake objective judgment as partisanship governs policy making. The imperative of justice too often tends to be subordinate to political preferences, as expediency responds to those interests. Human security is held subservient to national security, and the rule of law is replaced by the rule by force. People have become the means, and power the end. All of this stems from the decisions and actions of individuals, and the ripple effects of these decisions then spread across the global family.

Working for the United Nations for the past twenty-five years, I have seen this reality unfold as fact, which has had a profound impact on people's lives. Since 1988, my work has transported me to the war zones and crisis environments of those living on the edge of survival in Afghanistan, the Balkans and Darfur. It has brought me face to face with people living under occupation in Gaza and the West Bank, orphans lost in the forests of the Democratic Republic of the Congo, political prisoners struggling for freedom in Cambodia, families enduring daily violence in Guatemala and communities struggling with chronic crisis in Sudan. My work has also taken me behind doors into the structures and processes established to prevent and alleviate suffering, into the political chambers of the United Nations: the Security Council and the General Assembly.

This is not an account of my work in the United Nations, however. Rather, it is a recollection of the observations I have made in search for answers of a more universal nature, in the course of my personal and professional experience. The United Nations is a vitally important global organization with a noble mission that represents our shared weaknesses and strengths. It brings together the entire world and reflects the larger challenges and opportunities for humanity. Certain dynamics confront all individuals, societies and systems: the yearning for moral leadership, the desire for justice and freedom at international, national and individual levels; and, the deep longing for a more enlightened world. One that starts with ourselves, permeating our inner lives, our daily existence, and extending to our external positions and to our institutions.

But, we have not to date made connection between ourselves and the world at large, and grasped the big picture of this interconnection. In the words of the German philosopher, Immanuel Kant, "For peace to reign on Earth, humans must evolve into new beings who have learned to see the whole first."[4]

Numerous attempts have been made to come to grips with our compelling experience and purpose on earth as we struggle with wars, violence, injustice and inequity. At the organizational, political and diplomatic level, hundreds of documents have been produced to improve processes, design structural changes, articulate reforms and make the oft-repeated appeal for "political will." At the other end of the scale, the past decades have seen an impressive search for self-awareness and a purpose driven life at the individual level. Although they are interdependent, seldom do these two streams meet. The point of convergence has yet to crystalize.

Plato, the ancient Greek philosopher, alluded to this over 2000 years ago when he said: "There will be no end to the troubles of states, or of humanity itself, till philosophers become kings in this world, or till those we now call kings and rulers really and truly become philosophers, and political power and philosophy thus come into the same hands."[5] In the modern era, Robert Kennedy noted in the same spirit, "If more politicians knew poetry, and more poets knew politics, I am convinced the world would be a better place in which to live."[6]

The second United Nations Secretary-General, Dag Hammarskjold, echoed their observations. Hammarskjold, whom John F. Kennedy hailed as the "greatest statesman of our century," recognized the need to converge wisdom from around the globe and across history to find solutions to contemporary challenges. He suggested "the possibility of a synthesis of great traditions on which it is the task of our generation to build *one world*." [7]

In this book, I seek to illustrate the point of convergence. In doing so, I suggest the adoption of a new agenda and make the case for humanity. My goal is to take the analysis and debate to the next level – a level which has rarely been visited in the context of international politics, organizational culture and modern leadership. The intention is to transcend the barriers between politics, science, philosophy, psychology and spirituality, and distill the connection between our worldly institutions and our inner journey towards the power of humanity.

How is this to be done?

My experience on the frontlines, and in a large global organization, has shaped me. I have seen suffering, courage and the 'will to humanity' in its most compelling manifestations. But this is not a task for one person alone. So, in this book I have called on the help of over one hundred of the wisest personalities who have walked on earth. Among them are Gandhi, Martin Luther, Eleanor Roosevelt, Carl Jung, Mother Theresa, Lao Tzu and Anaïs Nin, as well as some of the unsung heroes whom I have met in my work.

I have gathered those persons together in a fictitious United Nations Security Council session on Humanity. The session has been called in answer to humanity's desperate needs at this crucial juncture in modern times. Responding to our collective cry, extraordinary political leaders, philosophers, humanitarians, scientists and writers have traveled through time and space to the United Nations Headquarters in New York City, to help us resolve contemporary challenges, set the standard for twenty-first century leadership, and offer a new and pioneering way forward in our own quest for growth and personal purpose.

We all have our flaws and make mistakes. The greatest minds of all time are no exceptions. However, their insightful understanding of the human condition remains extraordinary. In this book, I choose to focus on their predominantly positive traits. Their unique ability to maintain a larger vision and their sustained glimpses of the human potential will be distilled in support of the plea voiced at the first United Nations General Assembly session in 1946.

Blending my own experience and reflections with the timeless wisdom of others, the following debate – imagined on the floor of the

Security Council Chamber – seeks to connect the dots, unveil the bigger picture and depict our infinite human potential.

During the extraordinary session the wise share their insights. Every word remains their own, authentically quoted as they were once spoken, written or translated. A lawyer by training, I have taken the liberty to select their statements as they appear relevant in augmenting the case for humanity. Every chapter – each agenda item - is carefully structured to connect their insights, successively and gradually, to reveal some answers. The purpose is to illustrate the universality of their timeless wisdom, against my own experiences and reflections, breaking down the components that impact our humanity, piecing together a vision that will provide inspiration to overcome contemporary challenges and seize the opportunity to build *one world.*

This overarching opportunity is reflected in Gandhi's words: "The greatness of humanity is not in being human, but in being humane."8 He reminds us that the power of humanity is humanity itself. This is the highest human potential from which all else flows. While our potential begins in an inward journey and then blossoms outwardly, the intention of this book is to shed light from the outward to the inward. It is a journey from the mind to the soul wherein our own humanity resides.

"And you? When will you begin that long journey into yourself?" 9the poet Rumi asks. In the context of global affairs and the United Nations, this is the very same journey upon which Dag Hammarskjold traveled, summarized by the opening line of his posthumously published diary, *Markings*: "I am being driven forward into an unknown land."
The question – "And you?" – is one to which a growing number of us seek to respond.

We owe the journey into ourselves to the billions living at the receiving end of our tendency to yield to the 'will to power.' We also owe it to ourselves. I have discovered from those traveling on this journey that theirs is the power that ignites humanity, and it is their light that sustains it. May it also fuel and set ablaze ours.

*Yasmine Sherif*
*19 May 2015*

# Agenda Item 1
# Vision and Mission: Making the Connection

" *Vision without action is a daydream. Action without vision is a nightmare.* "

*Japanese proverb*

The cold winds of January sweep across the East River, driving through the towers of Manhattan. The sun peeks out behind the thirty-eight story United Nations building on First Avenue and 42nd Street. Today, the United Nations Security Council has convened an extraordinary session on Humanity.

There is a flurry of activity in the United Nations Secretariat. Agendas and talking points are being finalized. Staff, diplomats, activists and journalists scurry across the corridors and the open halls of the UN Secretariat to make final arrangements. The air is electric. Smiling faces mingle with skeptics, as the New York sun dances amidst the clouds.

The participants trickle into the Security Council Chamber. Abraham Lincoln and Mother Theresa arrive together. The legendary American President, who is 6'7," towers over Mother Theresa as they cross the plush carpet and pass the horseshoe table reserved for the United Nations Secretariat and the Permanent Missions of the fifteen-member Security Council. Leo Tolstoy, the Russian novelist, and Simone de Beauvoir, the French existentialist writer, are engaged in an amicable discussion as they take their seats. Nelson Mandela and Bertrand Russell, the British philosopher, entertain Hellen Keller, the blind and deaf author who went on to become one of our greatest humanists. She smiles as they guide her between them into the Chamber. Erich Fromm, the world renowned psychoanalyst and humanist philosopher, and Emily Dickinson, the famous poet, are immersed in serious conversation, while the former President of the Czech Republic, Vaclav Havel, walks behind them together with Socrates, the ancient Greek playwright, and Khalil Gibran, the Lebanese writer and poet.

It is a session the likes of which the world has never seen: truly, an unprecedented gathering. As these personalities stroll into the grand hall, I glance around. Faces from history books come alive. Amongst them, I see a face from the present.

In the crowd, I recognize a young man as he rolls into the Security Council Chamber in a wheelchair. His left leg is amputated, the other lifeless and badly burnt. Though his scars will never leave him, his almond-shaped green eyes radiate that striking light born out of gratitude for life. His name is Siddiqula. He is the Afghan boy I met in the hospital run by the International Committee of the Red Cross (ICRC) in Kabul, in the summer of 1991. The ambassadors of the Permanent Missions to the United Nations walk closely behind Siddiqula, their steps light and gentle. They are wary not to pass him, ready to assist.

By ten o'clock in the morning, the Chamber is filled to the brim. The President of the Council, a lifelong diplomat, has agreed to chair the session as an independent without any affiliation. He seats himself and pulls his papers together. As the session opens, we all know why we are here.

We have gathered here to assess how far we have come. The cry of humanity has summoned us for a mid term evaluation of the human family, and our shared aspirations. Today is a day for eternal truths. These are prerogatives that span over thousands of years, have stood the test of time and remain vitally relevant. Enlightened personalities, political leaders with moral authority, profound philosophers, insightful experts on the human mind, learned mystics and finally the rest of us – all the peoples of the United Nations – have come together in New York City. We have traveled from around the globe, and from time immemorial, to participate in this historical session – an extraordinary opportunity that will never return.

I look up at the rows of red and green seats in the gallery surrounding the Council members. As the last participants quietly stream in through the wide wooden doors, the remaining seats are rapidly filled. A hush descends, compelling us to contain our excitement. The President of the Council takes the floor.

Today's agenda is about humanity. It is no trivial subject. For the wise and reasonable person, it is too precious to be belittled, too profound to provoke pride, and too vital to all of us to invoke self-defense. Humanity begs us to speak the truth, and say what is necessary. At the same time, humanity seeks to be kind. For, we are all in this.

There is mood of both anticipation and trepidation in the Security Council Chamber. On the one hand, it is possible to sense a fear of condemnation; on the other, a yearning for inspiration. Bertrand Russell picks up on the dual energies in the Chamber. The founder of analytical philosophy leans towards Desmond Tutu, seated to his right, and whispers, "To save the world requires faith and courage: faith in reason and courage to proclaim what reason shows to be true."[10] Tutu, the Nobel Peace Prize Laureate whose struggle against apartheid in South Africa transformed him into a voice for the voiceless everywhere, smiles warmly at Russell and nods in agreement.

Watching them from across the Chamber, we sense that, today, there is no one present who is not ready to embrace truth, if that is what it takes to rescue the world from itself. Once more, we have hit a low point in our shared history. The old ways are weakening. The conventional methods of realpolitik have failed to bring peace and security to the world; our structures are becoming more rigid and, our perceptions narrower. Literally millions long for economic, social and political justice, while others search for purpose in their lives. And once again, we realize that it is only through truth that diversity and universal values will finally align. Just as several rivers merge into an ocean, the truth seamlessly brings oneness to our diversities. Only universal values can unify us. And only truth can set us free.

The first speaker, a tall white-haired man stands. He is dressed impeccably in an elegant suit and tie - his sartorial trademark. He tilts towards the podium and nods at the President. As he requests the floor, all heads turn in his direction. Only some knew him. He was once expected to be a world teacher, thanks to his insightful understanding of human nature and its interconnection to global challenges. But he rejected such enticements, and resisted any attempt to elevate him. From then on, his wisdom blew freely as a wind of inspiration, touching and teaching millions. The great Indian mystic and writer, Jiddu Krishnamurti, takes the floor: "We, as individuals, as human beings, in whatever part of the world we happen to live or whatever culture we happen to belong to, are totally responsible for the whole state of the world."[11] He stops for a moment. His penetrating eyes, reflecting deeply seated wisdom, wander around the Chamber before he resumes, "And as we are – the world is." [12] Krishnamurti quietly takes his seat.

As I watch from afar, Ralph Waldo Emerson, the American essayist and poet, appears behind Krishnamurti and complements his statement, "The reason why the world lacks unity, and lies broken and in heaps, is because man is disunited with himself,"[13] Emerson says, as he finds a free chair.

The rest of us, seated in the Chamber, reflect on their opening remarks. Their words remind us of the inextricable relationship between the individual and the world. There is a deep interdependence between what we think, say and do, and the actual state of the world. While this connection may not be easily discerned at first sight, we cannot miss its everyday manifestations. Violence, oppression and discrimination start with one individual thought, which multiplies and influences the surroundings; be it a group, a society or a nation. By the same law of interdependence, one person's 'will to power' - or another's 'will to humanity' - shapes or alters the course of institutions, politics and nations.

As the first speakers make their statements, I sit and listen, alongside the rest of humanity. The speakers have the authority of insight, I think to myself. What about the rest of us? Nietzsche rightly said that we are predominantly driven by the 'will to power,' and now we wrestle with its consequences.

We race ahead bewildered by the sheer pace we have set. We don't notice the disconnection - either within ourselves or in our relationship to the world outside. Blinded by the illusion of power, we are guided by shortsightedness. By daily and habitual choices, often seemingly routine and unrelated, we fail to attend to the call of humanity. The words of Dr. Zuleta Angel reappear before us:

*In this we shall not fail. An inner voice tells us that, animated by a broad and sincere feeling for humanity, we can lift up our hearts...*

The plea of the first United Nations General Assembly in 1946 still lies in waiting.

Silence seeps through the Chamber. In an ordinary setting on an ordinary day, some may consider the opening statements to be too simplistic or even sentimental in an official setting of this kind. But mere perceptions do not suffice today to render invalid the stark authenticity of Krishnamurti's and Emerson's testimonials. Today the question warrants an answer: can there be a different society? Out of necessity, the founders of the United Nations determined that this was indeed possible. In 1945, leaders of the world gathered in San Francisco to start anew. They had a vision, and a deeply felt commitment to bring about a better world.

"We believed. There was a spirit of hope and idealism in the air," the British Ambassador, Archie Mackenzie, told me when we met in New York City in 2003. He was present at the signing of the UN Charter in San Francisco in 1945. Almost sixty years later I had the privilege of inviting Ambassador Mackenzie to lecture to my students at Long Island University, where I taught classes on the United Nations and human rights in international politics. I was inspired by Ambassador Mackenzie's belief in the untapped potential of the United Nations. During our encounter, over half a century after the signing of the UN Charter in San Francisco, he inspired a new generation of students aspiring to serve with the same universal values and commitment.

Today, Mackenzie shares the insights he has gained into the global organization he once helped create. As he stands to speak, he greets everyone in the Chamber with a polite and friendly nod, "The UN needs a moral and spiritual dynamic to help it deal with such basic human weaknesses as hatred, cynicism, corruption and egotism, and to enable it to tap into higher sources of wisdom. And of course, in such a spiritual odyssey there is another categorical imperative that applies: 'everyone must start with themselves.'[14]

Recognizing our interdependence, the United Nations Charter of 1945 enshrined an ethical philosophy and sense for justice that epitomized the spirit of the founders of the world body. Despite the differences and diversity of its founders, the Charter resulted in a shared sense of humanity and universal values; our common and unquestionable truth:

> *To save succeeding generations from the scourge of war, which twice in our lifetime has brought untold sorrow to mankind, and*
> *To reaffirm faith in fundamental human rights, in the dignity and worth of the human person, in the equal rights of men and women and of nations large and small, and*
> *To establish conditions under which justice and respect for the obligations arising from treaties and other sources of international law can be maintained, and*
> *To promote social progress and better standards of life in larger freedom.*

Seventy years later, we ask ourselves how far we have come. Progress has been made in certain areas. We have brought self-determination to *almost* all people, made some economic progress and developed international law, among other things. We have also failed in some very critical areas. We have not achieved global peace and security, nor universal respect for human rights. Since 1945, we have seen over 200 armed conflicts, and more than twenty million lives lost. 90% of those who have died have been civilians. Each life represents a loss of humanity.

Most, if not all, contemporary armed conflicts are marked by crimes against humanity. Millions were killed in the genocides in Cambodia and Rwanda. Syria's armed conflict has claimed over 220,000 dead, and has led to over ten million people being displaced from their homes. The people of Afghanistan have suffered thirty-six years of war, while the Palestinian people have endured nearly fifty years under military occupation. Dreaming of freedom and human rights, billions continue to live amidst violence and abject poverty. *They* – the billions who suffer – constitute both our vision, and our mission, as enshrined in the United Nations Charter and international conventions.

Against this reality, the most essential question we can ask ourselves today is whether we are connected with, and aligned to, our vision and mission? In the muddy waters of the mundane and routine, our quest for *larger freedom* under the United Nations Charter often plays out within the boundaries of traditional hierarchies and uninspiring power struggles. Frequently, our search for justice gets entangled in political interests, and is diverted from international law and universal values. Not without a sense of growing frustration, we ask ourselves whether impersonal bureaucracies and *realpolitik* have sneaked upon us from behind, fracturing our dream for humankind.

"I have tried to resist the forces of bureaucratic inertia. In the corridors of diplomacy people gradually tend to lose their capacity to distinguish between what is important and what isn't. A phrase or a comma in a draft resolution suddenly comes to assume disproportionate importance," says Prince Sadruddin Aga Khan, a former senior United

Nations official, speaking candidly, "Negotiations go on for hours, for nights on end, before agreement is reached on what is generally the lowest common denominator. You feel that you have won a great victory. But no one will read the text which was so difficult to draft."[15]

Sadruddin Aga Khan knows well the challenges we face. He joined the world body at the age of twenty-one, and served millions of refugees and the most downtrodden throughout his lifetime. He sees the interconnection between our structures and the state of the world. His message is simple, "It is now widely and rightly accepted that we live in a world which is more interdependent than ever before, and that problems are increasingly global in character. At the risk of stating the obvious, I would say that when governments realize that certain problems are beyond their powers, it is clear that the United Nations has an irreplaceable role to play. At the same time, the world is changing considerably and the United Nations must change too." [16]

After a distinguished career as the United Nations High Commissioner for Refugees (UNHCR), Sadruddin Aga Khan assumed leadership of the United Nations Office for the Coordination of Economic and Humanitarian Assistance to Afghanistan (UNOCHA), following the withdrawal of Soviet troops in 1989. As a new law graduate, I had just joined his office in Geneva.

Sadruddin Aga Khan was a dynamic leader, cultured and compassionate, who chose to serve, rather than to be served. His door was always open, and his weekly staff meetings included a *tour de table,* in which all staff irrespective of their roles, were invited to actively contribute and offer their insights.

It was in one of those staff meetings that I, a young lawyer and amateur poet, suggested that we use poetry to advocate for the plight of the Afghan people. It was an unusual proposal, and I feared I had made a fool of myself. My colleagues looked at each other in an embarrassing silence. To my relief, however, Sadruddin Aga Khan was quick to respond, "Yasmine is right. Poetry can change the world."

His response mirrored the spirit of the founders of the United Nations. The Charter of 1945 and the Universal Declaration of Human Rights of 1948 are both crafted poetically. The inspiring preamble of the Declaration is not the work of a technocratic mindset. It was crafted by those able to delve into their hearts and souls, to express a dream shared by billions. Just as poets do.

It was a magnificent manifestation of the 'will to humanity.' Inspired by East and West, North and South, and treading in the footprints of the American Bill of Rights and the Declaration of Human Rights of the French Revolution, the first lines of the preamble of the United Nations Universal Declaration of Human Rights read:

> *Whereas recognition of the inherent dignity and of the equal and inalienable rights of all members of the human family is the foundation of freedom, justice and peace in the world,*
> *Whereas disregard and contempt for human rights have resulted in barbarous acts which have outraged the conscience of mankind, and the advent of a world in which human beings shall enjoy freedom of speech and belief and freedom from fear and want has been proclaimed as the highest aspiration of the common people,*
> *Whereas it is essential, if man is not to be compelled to have recourse, as a last resort, to rebellion against tyranny and oppression, that human rights should be protected by the rule of law.../....*
> *Whereas it is essential to promote the development of friendly relations between nations,*
> *Whereas the peoples of the United Nations have in the Charter reaffirmed their faith in fundamental human rights, in the dignity and worth of the human person and in the equal rights of men and women and have determined to promote social progress and better standards of life in larger freedom...*

Eleanor Roosevelt, together with the French lawyer, Rene Cassin, was the driving force behind the Universal Declaration for Human Rights, which was adopted by the United Nations General Assembly in 1948. Composed of thirty articles, the Universal Declaration enshrines values for the human family at large; such as the right to due process, equality before the law, freedom of conscience and freedom of expression, the right to work and education, the prohibition against torture and the principle of nondiscrimination.

These universally recognized rights, and several more, were eventually embodied in numerous legally binding conventions, such as the Covenant on Civil and Political Rights and the Covenant on Economic, Social and Cultural Rights, both of which were adopted by the General Assembly in 1966.

With the Charter, the Universal Declaration and successive conventions which comprise international law, one can safely say that the United Nations was not established to find consensus around the lowest common denominator. It was created to inspire and mold consensus around the highest of human values.

The onus was laid on all of us: the United Nations Member States and we, the peoples of the United Nations, especially those among us professing to serve. Yet, almost a century later, these universal rights are neither largely respected nor applied equally. The essence of the law has given way to impunity and selectivity. These two doctrines have become all too common bargaining chips in international affairs.

The departure from our vision and mission is the result of many small and big decisions. Whether it has been influenced by national interests and geopolitical alliances or simply by organizational processes in our offices and conference rooms, there is always an individual and individual interest lying beneath selectivity, inaction and inertia. By default, decisions steered by the 'will to power' tend to weaken our universal values, while decisions guided by the 'will to humanity' naturally strengthen them.

"Sometimes I wonder if we shall ever grow up in our politics and say definite things which mean something, or whether we shall always go on using generalities to which everyone can subscribe, and which mean little." [17]Eleanor Roosevelt emerges from the audience. Standing tall in the first row, she speaks with well-earned authority and raises her voice, "When will our conscience grow so tender that we will act to prevent human misery rather than avenge it?" [18]

Her question is rhetorical. It is one to which we all know the answer. A conscientious choice is one that safeguards the rights of all without discrimination - the cornerstone of the Universal Declaration of Human Rights and international law. In the spirit of the United Nations, and based on the notion of *natural law*,[19] these rights are inherent in human nature, and underpin the universally shared ethos of *the golden rule*: to do to others what we want others to do to us.

"When you are laboring for others, let it be with the same zeal as if it were for yourself,"[20] a voice calls out softly from the audience. Confucius has just spoken. He leans back in his chair. I look around for someone who personifies Confucius's call, and spot General Roméo Dallaire in a corner of the Chamber.

General Dallaire was the Canadian Force Commander who led the United Nations Assistance Mission in Rwanda (UNAMIR). A tiny country in the horn of Africa, Rwanda suffered an atrocious genocide in the spring of 1994. Some 900,000 human beings were systematically slaughtered like sheep with machetes by their neighbors, classmates and friends.

During this dark era, General Dallaire made repeated calls for intervention to save lives. His pleas went unheard by individuals above him. From their point of view, they lacked the "political will," resources and mandate to intervene. In response, General Dallaire rose to the occasion. He made a personal decision to save as many lives as possible without "political will," resources or mandate. He stepped far beyond his call of duty, and is credited with having saved 32,000 lives. He worked for others with the same zeal as if for himself.

General Dallaire takes the floor and speaks authoritatively, "Rwanda will never ever leave me. It's in the pores of my body. My soul is in those hills, my spirit is with the spirits of all those people who were slaughtered and killed that I know of, and many that I didn't know."[21] He rests his face in his palms and pauses for a moment.

After a brief reflection on the lesson learned, he resumes, "As the nineties drew to a close and the new millennium dawned with no sign of an end to these ugly little wars, it was as if each troubling conflict we were faced with had to pass the test of whether we could "care" about it or "identify" with the victims before we'd get involved."[22]

In the aftermath of his life-changing experience, Dallaire asks poignantly: "Are all humans human? Or are some more human than others?"[23] Dallaire decided to carry the banner of the United Nations founding principles when others turned away. His decision to act in the face of heart-wrenching suffering and danger, epitomized the meaning of true service: while service for humanity might be a noble endeavor, nobler still is service *with* humanity.

"You may choose to look the other way but you can never say again that you did not know."[24] I hear another voice, and turn my head to trace its owner. It is William Wilberforce. A uniquely self-critical politician, Wilberforce underwent a powerful personal metamorphosis which led him to transform the lives of millions. His conversion inspired his humanitarian reform, which in turn led to the abolishment of slavery in England with the passing of the Slave Trade Act in 1807.

A British politician who led the campaign for the abolition of slavery for twenty-six years and succeeded, Wilberforce continues, "Wherever we direct our view, we discover the melancholy proofs of our depravity; whether we look to ancient or modern times, to barbarous or civilized nations, to the conduct of the world around us, or to the monitor within the breast; whether we read, or hear, or act, or think, or feel, the same humiliating lesson is forced upon us.[25] Great indeed are our opportunities; great also is our responsibility. If to be feelingly alive to the sufferings of my fellow-creatures is to be a fanatic, I am one of the most incurable fanatics ever permitted to be at large,"[26] Wilberforce concludes his statement and retreats to his chair.

The speakers' remarks spark an internal inquiry: are our challenges so great that only those fully humane have the capacity to end inhumanity of such breadth and magnitude? It takes empathy to step into someone else's shoes and understand what needs to be done; it requires courage to defy politically and socially accepted norms of complacency; audacity to make tough decisions that challenge rigid structures; and, ultimately, self-awareness and humility to transform one's being into a tool of service.

"Work for something because it is good, not just because it stands a chance to succeed,"[27] Vaclav Havel says as he stands and gazes across the Chamber, "We still don't know how to put morality ahead of politics, science, and economics. We are still incapable of understanding that the only genuine backbone of our actions - if they are to be moral - is responsibility: responsibility to something higher than my family, my country, my firm, my success."[28]

Havel, who walked the long and testing road from being a dissident and political prisoner to the president of a nation, continues, "Man's attitude towards the world must be radically changed. We have to abandon the arrogant belief that the world is merely a puzzle to be solved, a machine with instructions for use waiting to be discovered. We must return to the values that define us as humans, and on which everyday interaction is based. Practiced, these values become 'living truth' and they must be the values of every citizen and of any politician.'"[29]

Silence ensues as the Chamber reflects on the observations that have been made. We see the connection between ourselves, the institutions we serve, and the societies we create. Our structures and systems are not abstract and anonymous entities. The world is not a fictional movie. In the real world, our institutions and policies are the product of the human component making up those entities and articulating those policies. This human component cannot afford to lose its human quality. If it does, the structures themselves lose their humanity. It is people who project values and who make moral choices and responsible decisions. And yet, as we try to improve our responses to poverty, violence and all forms of injustice, we have made the decision to reform our structures but not to change our own attitudes. We seek to make our processes more effective, our procedures more efficient. But when do we work with ourselves to become more humane?

"Our society is run by a managerial bureaucracy, by professional politicians," says Erich Fromm, the world renowned psychiatrist and humanist as he rises from his chair. Fromm, whose greatest work *Escape from Freedom* is the founding pillar of political psychology, speaks from a place of intellectual honesty, "People are motivated by mass suggestion, their aim is producing more and consuming more, as purposes in themselves. All activities are subordinated to economic goals, means have become ends; man is an automaton — well fed, well clad, but without any ultimate concern for that which is his peculiarly human quality and function." [30] Fromm's voice is firm as he shares his insight into the quietly desperate mindsets possessed by millions who walk a tedious track.

Lord Maynard Keynes can be seen across the aisle. Tweaking his well-trimmed mustache, he listens attentively. Considered the greatest economist of the twentieth century, Lord Keynes requests the floor. He glances at Fromm to signal agreement and reinforces the wisdom just shared, "The day is not far off when the Economic Problem will take the back seat where it belongs, and the area of heart and head will be occupied where it belongs, or reoccupied by our real problems, the problems of life and human relations, of creation, and of behavior and religion." [31]

While listening, I, like so many others present, gather my thoughts. I wonder if a day is possible when we no longer glance at the surface, but choose to penetrate the shell and see things far more deeply. A day when we recognize that politics, economics, or the rule of law cannot be divorced from the essence of our humanity and our universal values.

It is then that we will realize that a world in which 1% owns 40% of the planet's wealth [32] is the result of exclusive competition rather than creative empowerment; that national interests clashing with universal values result in a clash between civilizations, and not the reverse. It is then that we shall recognize that restructuring our offices and business processes are mere surface gestures, and cannot be substituted for re-constructing ourselves. When we make the connection between ourselves, our vision and mission, we will break through the illusion and see reality for what it is.

"The most important of all revolutions is a revolution in senti-ments, manners and moral opinions,"[33] exclaims Edmund Burke, the British statesman and politician. Like the speakers before him, he does not shy away from the hard truth.

Vaclav Havel nods at Keynes and Burke, and stands to make a longer point, reaffirming the acuity of their remarks, "Without a global revolution in the sphere of human consciousness, nothing will change for the better in the sphere of our being as humans, and the catastro-phe toward which this world is headed - be it ecological, social, demo-graphic or a general breakdown of civilization - will be unavoidable. [34]

He pauses for a moment of reflection and then concludes his statement, "We are still incapable of understanding that the only genu-ine backbone of all our actions, if they are to be moral, is responsibility. Even a purely moral act that has no hope of any immediate and visible political effect can gradually and indirectly, over time, gain in political significance."[35]

Havel speaks of ethical politics. He pleads for a more profound sense of moral responsibility and the power of universal values in pol-itics. He confirms through his own example of forbearance that we shape political reality. As a politician, he reminds us that the heights we can achieve for humanity largely depend on the depths we have explored within ourselves. Ethical politics is not only desirable. It is possible.

Havel's words stand in sharp contrast to the prevailing assumption that we must adjust to a political reality lacking in universal values and moral courage. It is precisely this kind of short-sightedness that has brought about such a political reality.

"It is when we all play it safe that we create a world of utmost insecurity," Dag Hammarskjold notes, remaining in his seat. [36]

All of us listening can discern that these visionary thinkers have served us with the truth.

There is an alternative political reality to the one we have created. It is an alternative that the founders of the United Nations envisioned. It is a political reality where the 'will to power' yields to the 'will to humanity.'

Albert Einstein, who has quietly observed the discussion up to now, reaches for his microphone, "We cannot solve our problems with the same thinking we used when we created them. In fact, insanity is to do the same things over and over again and expect a different result."[37] He leans forward and offers a deeper analysis, "The ill success, despite their obvious sincerity, of all the efforts made during the last decade to reach this goal leaves us no room to doubt that strong psychological factors are at work, which paralyzes these efforts."[38]

The debate is beginning to penetrate the shell. Others join in and take it further. We hold our breaths in anticipation.

"Fear, greed, and the desire for power are the psychological motivating forces not only behind warfare and violence between nations, tribes, religions, and ideologies, but also the cause of incessant conflict in personal relationships,"[39] says Eckhart Tolle, the Cambridge educated bestselling author of *A New Earth.* He speaks with a calm and soothing voice. We listen attentively.

Seated next to him, Abraham Maslow, the prominent psychologist, signals consent and takes the floor. He sheds further light on the psychological forces at work to which Einstein and Tolle have just referred, "Let people realize clearly that every time they threaten someone or humiliate or unnecessarily hurt or dominate or reject another human being, they become forces for the creation of psychopathology, even if these be small forces," he says and continues, "Let them recognize that every person who is kind, helpful, decent, psychologically democratic, affectionate, and warm, is a psychotherapeutic force, even though a small one."[40] With characteristic effortlessness, Maslow draws the threads of the debate together.

The Security Council reflects on the statements made, all of them atypical of the regular debates. Despite, or perhaps thanks to, the depth of the discussion, the atmosphere is light. The burden of political correctness is lifted, the heavy weight of conformity removed. Business as usual is not the order of the day. This is a day of reflection by the wisest minds of the ages. There is a fork in the road. We have choices to make. We may be uncertain and, understandably, also cynical. But, we all know that something deeper, higher and far greater is required from us.

As the first item on the agenda winds down, Krishnamurti reappears to bring the debate to its conclusion. He climbs the stairs to the top row, in order to face all the participants. In closing, he sums up the comments that have been made heretofore and offers a way forward.

"There is a common relationship between us all. We are the world essentially, basically, fundamentally. The world is you, and you are the world. Realizing that fundamentally, deeply, not romantically, not intellectually but actually, then we see that our problem is a global problem. It is not my problem or your particular problem, it is a human problem. Governments want efficient technicians, not human beings, because human beings become dangerous to governments. But, we disregard a whole field which has yet to be discovered, which may alter a whole worlds' work."[41]

The time has come to step bravely into this field and to tread the path.

# Agenda Item 2
# Leadership and Power:
# Empowering Others

*" If your actions inspire others to dream more, learn more, do more and become more, you are a leader. "*

*John Quincy Adams*

The participants trail into the Chamber after a short coffee break at the Delegates' Lounge - the UN café and bar with a panoramic view of northern Manhattan. The President of the Council strikes twice on the table with his gavel. He calls the Chamber to order and invites Leo Tolstoy to launch the discussion under the next agenda item.

Once described by his teachers as 'unable or unwilling' to learn, Tolstoy, the legendary Russian novelist, went on to inspire great leaders for humanity, such as Gandhi and Martin Luther King, Jr. Now, he takes the floor and remarks in the spirit of his own honest search for truth, "Love of power is not connected with goodness but with qualities that are the opposite of goodness, such as pride, cunning and cruelty[42]."

His opening statement reverberates across the Chamber. Aristotle looks up from his pad. The stern faced ancient Greek philosopher places his palms on the table in front him. A thin smile cracks the veneer of severity on his face, as he nods affirmatively at Tolstoy and exclaims aloud: "No man loves the man whom he fears."[43]

Together, they have set the tone.

The President of the Council takes a sip of water from his glass and invites the participants to contemplate the opening remarks. The question before us concerns the leadership of the twenty-first century. What kind of leadership will blaze the trail into the unknown field and chart a new way forward? Our children need role models, our youth need mentors and the rest of us need to set an example.

"Our chief want is someone who inspires us to be what we know we could be,"[44] Ralph Waldo Emerson suggests, softly, as if still in thought.

Charged by his enticing statement, we listen attentively and prod further. Who are the leaders that will unleash our potential and uplift humanity? Will they be those seeking or succumbing to power? Will they be the shrewd, the cunning or the cruel?

Albert Einstein raises his eyebrows as if the questions are superfluous. They are, indeed. Though he knows a response may not be necessary since we all have an idea of the answer, he decides to make a point and stands, "Blind belief in authority is the greatest enemy of truth.[45] Force always attracts men of low morality."[46] As the grinning scientist sits down, the Chamber considers his bold comment.

His statement is not one of righteousness, but one of right before might. "Low morality" does not necessarily mean lack of morals or values. Most human beings possess some sense of ethics and values - as long as those imperatives do not cause confrontation with authority and power; as long as there is no sacrifice of personal and national interests. "Low morality," as Einstein phrased it, means treating ethics and universal values as subordinate to authority, power and partisanship. Often it leads to trading principles for a place in the comfort zone. At other times, it means losing our ability to discriminate and our good judgment, in the fog of fear that separates right from wrong. Eventually, the consequences catch up with us. Although we may not see it as we race ahead, bending or clapping, the impact is far-reaching.

When we compromise universal values and international law, when we clap to the drums of war, or silently bend before an injustice, we hurt the truth - the very heart that pounds for our humanity. Blind belief in authority or power cannot liberate others, it cannot set that truth free.

We grapple with organizational, social and political challenges – often as a consequence of the 'will to power.' At the same time, we are wired not to question power. So, we adopt a blind belief in authority, as Einstein phrased it. This is evidenced in the gulf between a magnificent vision and the kind of leadership it warrants. We get the leaders we deserve - not necessarily the leaders able or willing to truly serve.

Yet, serving *with* humanity requires extraordinary leaders. For, in the dark abyss where the downtrodden reside, the abnormal has become "normal," and abnormal problems require extraordinary solutions. But leadership largely based on authority and power tends to be disconnected from the people it serves. Such leaders often reduce people to numbers, producing ordinary solutions at best, and callous solutions at worst.

"A good decision is based on knowledge and not on numbers",[47] says Plato, who over 2000 years ago, laid the foundation for Western philosophy and science but whose wisdom is just as relevant today. If we cannot relate to the humanity in people, but look down on persons merely as numbers or means, how can we possibly aspire to lift up all of humanity?

"Anyone who conducts an argument by appealing to authority is not using his intelligence; he is just using his memory,"[48] nods Leonardo da Vinci, the unsurpassed genius, whose multifaceted talents have dignified the world with exquisite beauty and dazzling knowledge.

Abraham Maslow smiles in agreement, "If you only have a hammer, you tend to see every problem as a nail."[49]

Their insights hit the target. Shortsightedness seldom does. Leaders driven by the 'will to power' tend to place power above values, obedience above moral courage and, national interests above the human family. We look at each other across the Chamber. In a moment of clarity, we connect the dots: who then is left to serve *with* humanity?

Abraham Lincoln rises, deliberately, from his chair. His struggle against the establishment of slavery cost him political power in 1858. Yet his commitment to end slavery persisted and returned him to power two years later, making him one of the most remarkable of U.S presidents. Standing erect, Lincoln now speaks to the Council, "Nearly all men can stand adversity, but if you want to test a man's character, give him power."[50] Setting an example, his leadership brought an end to slavery changing the lives of millions and redirecting the course of history. As Lincoln returns to his seat, we are afforded a few moments of quiet reflection.

The Dutch philosopher, Baruch Spinoza, breaks the silence. He leans over his microphone and announces his wish to elaborate further on the statements just made, "The ultimate aim of government is not to rule, or restrain by fear, nor to exact obedience, but to free every man from fear that he may live in all possible security," he proclaims. "In fact the true aim of government is liberty,"[51] he concludes in a soft and humble voice, both characteristic of the man.

Spinoza, one of the greatest of Western philosophers and author of *Ethics*, in which he contends that ethics is just as logical as mathematics, reminds us of the responsibility that rests with every leader and governing structure: not to rule by fear, or to aim at obedience or conformity, but rather to liberate people.

The Chamber listens in awe of this amazing philosopher who refused to entertain fear of authority, despite being ostracized by his contemporaries for exploring controversial ideas. His words shine a clear light on the essence of leadership. Healthy and enlightened leadership emphasizes humanity before authority, or "live one day at a time, emphasizing ethics rather than rules,"[52] Dr. Wayne Dyer, the world renowned psychologist and bestselling author, suggests from his seat in the gallery.

I am instantly attracted to the gist of Dyer's remarks, so typical of his inspiring works, which I have read since I was a law student in the 1980s. As a lawyer, I can relate to the notion that ethics stands above rules. People are the end. The law is the means. Not the contrary. Leadership can no longer mean resorting to rules to control people. What we need today are leaders who are driven by ethics to protect people under the law.

"At a time of intensifying global anxiety, I believe the people of the world are crying out for profound and inspiring leadership equal to the challenge we face,"[53] Prince Zeid bin Ra'ad, the United Nations High Commissioner for Human Rights, states.

Bin Ra'ad was instrumental in the establishment of the Rome Statute and the International Criminal Court (ICC). Mandated to uphold international law, the most essential objective of the ICC is to deliver justice to those suffering war crimes, crimes against humanity and genocide. It represents a step forward in establishing a world order based on the rule of law, as opposed to one based on the rule by force. "To rescue our planet we need more compassionate and wise people piloting our collective fate,"[54] bin Ra'ad concludes. He calls for leaders fit for that purpose.

We stand at a crossroads. The twenty-first century needs leaders able to connect the vision to the mission, leaders who translate international law and universal values into action, not just on paper, to paraphrase George Bernard Shaw's opening remarks. As stewards of moral courage, those leaders must chart our collective fate forward for the human family at large. They know that the road to achieve universal values is paved with moral choices. They have the courage to make those choices, and enable others to make the same choices. Driven by the 'will to humanity,' they understand that power, in its most humane sense, is a precious privilege to empower others, not just themselves, or their own, but all.

"If we look ahead into the next century, leaders will be those who empower others,"[55] says Bill Gates as he appears from the audience. The founder of Microsoft and business magnate speaks from a place of direct experience. He shares his wealth across the world through creative empowerment. As of 2013, Bill Gates had donated some $28 billion, approximately 43% of his net worth, to empower people around the globe to lift themselves out of poverty and inequality. He now looks across the Chamber and beyond, as if gazing into the new century, "Great teachers have the power to change the world."[56]

One of them is José Ramos-Horta. Since the independence of East Timor in 2002, the Nobel Peace Prize Laureate has served in several leadership positions in his country: as Foreign Minister, Prime Minister and President. I first met Ramos-Horta at the United Nations Headquarters in New York in 2000, when he was still struggling for independence for East Timor. From there ensued a long lasting friendship, which for me was a treasured source of knowledge about the humility and the perseverance with which extraordinary leaders serve in the face of great obstacles and tragic personal loss. Ramos-Horta's lack of self-pity, and his deep empathy for others, can't be ignored. Those qualities embed his thoughts, words and actions. His leadership is not just one of appointment, but one that has been earned along the path of sacrifice.

During one of my visits to East Timor in the summer of 2010, Ramos-Horta and I drove around Dili in his modest open pickup. He waved to his people and took time to speak to everyone on the streets of the capital. Witnessing the abundant affection displayed by the East Timorese people towards their President - the human touch as they greeted each other, the smiles they shared - I asked President Ramos-Horta to define the most important traits in a leader. Without hesitation he replied, "It is not about academic degrees, nor the awards we receive. It is about compassion, a golden heart. But that alone is not enough. We also need wisdom. Put the two together... and it is about humanity."

Leaders driven by the 'will to humanity' have wisdom bestowed upon them. They see things from afar. They recognize the correlation between themselves, the state of the world and universal values. They know that ideals can only be realized where thoughts, words and actions consistently align with the vision. For, as Gandhi said, "One cannot do right in one department of life, whilst occupied in wrongdoing in any other department. Life is one indivisible whole."[57]

They *become* the vision.
Those leaders shoulder responsibility to change themselves in the process of changing the world. Or, to paraphrase Gandhi's well-known words, "Be the change you wish to see." Like carefully fitted stepping stones, each seemingly small decision supports the bigger picture. Such leaders gradually transform into walking ethics, living principles.

"A just person is one who is conformed and transformed into justice,"[58] Meister Eckhart, the German theologian and mystic, concludes my silent contemplation. I look up and around.

Appropriately, Dag Hammarskjold now takes the floor. I turn my head to catch a glimpse of Hammarskjold who is seated further down the row. His voice is gentle, his demeanor confident, "Only he deserves power who every day justifies it,"[59] he states and then continues, "Dare he, for whom circumstances make it possible to realize his true destiny, refuse it simply because he is not prepared to give up everything else."[60] He stops for a moment. Hammarskjold weighs his words carefully. He is about to set the standards: "A true leader, a civil servant, is an active instrument, a catalyst, perhaps an inspirer – he serves."[61]

Hammarskjold protected the universal values of the United Nations rigorously, and was a staunch advocate of international law. His posthumously published collection of personal and philosophical notations, *Markings*, helps us to understand the profound depths he plumbed to become the person we saw. Hammarskjold's inner journey and global statesmanship personified the profound meaning of ethical leadership: a leader conferred with power ultimately has to give up the small self, the ego, to gain access to the more profound qualities of the larger self, such as integrity. Just as the 'will to power' and the 'will to humanity' do not reconcile, the ego and integrity are diametrically opposed. One has to give way for the other.

"Your position never gives you the right to command. It only imposes on you the duty of so living your life that others may receive your orders without being humiliated"[62] Hammarskjold notes, as he finishes. He reminds us that out of integrity comes humility - the capacity to honor the humanity in others.

As we digest the words just spoken, the great philosopher and poet of ancient China, Lau Tzu, rises from his chair and expounds further. Weaving together the delicate threads of profound wisdom shared by previous speakers, Lau Tzu speaks calmly and slowly, "He who controls others may be powerful, but he who has mastered himself is mightier still,"[63] he says, delicately choosing his words, "I have three precious things which I hold fast and prize. The first is gentleness; the second is frugality; the third is humility, which keeps me from putting myself before others. Be gentle and you can be bold; be frugal and you can be liberal; avoid putting yourself before others and you can become a leader among men."[64]

Lau Tzu stops for a moment. He looks at the podium and up at the rows, before resuming with an appeal to all those present, "If you want to lead the people, you must learn how to follow them." [65] He pauses for a moment to allow us to absorb his words, "A leader is best when people barely know he exists, when his work is done, his aim fulfilled, they will say: we did it ourselves."[66] Walking the earth thousands of years before us, Lau Tzu, the founder of Taoism, speaks from realms that conventional leadership can barely fathom. He defines the true meaning of empowerment. We can scarcely believe that such a man and wisdom existed so long ago.

"Let us show great humility towards the peoples we wish to help, for we have very little to teach them."[67] A voice is heard behind me. It is

Sadruddin Aga Khan, who served millions of refugees, whose lives were seared by the stoic struggle for survival amidst war, famine and persecution.

Lao Tzu tilts his head in agreement, "Go to the people. Live with them. Learn from them. Love them."[68]

The Council is quiet. We reflect with a hint of embarrassment. They touch the core of leadership driven by the 'will to humanity.' As leaders they did not primarily love to lead, but lead with love. They knew that a genuine power to serve is amplified by softening the heart. The more we empathize with those we serve, the more we empower them, the more powerful is our response. The desire to empower others is born out of love; *feeling* their suffering which we cannot fully fathom, and *seeing* their strength which we do not fully possess.

"Those who want to do good knock at the gate; those who love find the gate open,"[69] Rabindranath Tagore whispers, while gazing at the horseshoe table. The iconic Indian poet, and Nobel Prize Laureate in Literature, shares his aphorism of a higher logic that is so relevant to leadership and service.

Together, the speakers have described the spirit of serving *with* humanity.

Leaders of the twenty-first century make the connection. Their minds are expansive enough to capture the vision; their hearts empathetic enough to feel for people and, their souls have been sensitized enough to connect the two through the right actions. They inspire us to *become fully humane* to paraphrase Gandhi. Those leaders become catalysts for *setting others free*. They find the gate open. In the process, those leaders free themselves and the world in the same instant. They set the truth free.

The President of the Council takes note. He smiles reassuringly, for he knows the temptations of skepticism. As he sums up the session, his head turns towards the participants who are present from history. He glances at them with reverence and gratitude, because today, we are assembled amongst leaders and personalities whose lifetime achievements and legacies testify to the possibility of such leadership. They steered our way forward with compassion and wisdom. Fit for purpose, these are the leaders who lit the path courageously and aroused in others the 'will to humanity.'

As the discussion draws to a close, the President invites another personality to offer his final remarks. The Indian mystic Swami Vivekananda rises slowly from his chair. Instrumental in bringing Eastern philosophy, faith and awareness to the West, Vivekananda influenced and inspired many great minds, such as Nikola Tesla, Mahatma Gandhi and Leo Tolstoy.

His voice dancing with a charming lilt, Vivekananda speaks to the Chamber, "What we want is the human being who is harmoniously developed. We want women and men whose heart feels intensely the miseries and sorrows of the world; the human being who not only can feel but can find the meaning of things, who delves deeply into the heart of nature and understanding; the human being who will not even stop there, who wants to work. Such combination of head, heart and hand is what we want." [70] Vivekananda retreats into silence for a moment, before closing the session, "Why not the giant who is equally active, equally knowing, and equally loving? Is it impossible? Certainly not - this is the man of the future....." [71]

This is the leader of the twenty-first century.

# Agenda Item 3

# *Values and Justice:*
# *Appealing to the Essence*

*"*
*Justice is conscience. Not a personal conscience, but the conscience of the whole of humanity. "*

*Aleksandr Solzhenitsyn*

"The only thing necessary for evil to prevail is for good individuals to do nothing" [72] I well remember the day that Edmund Burke's words rang out in the Security Council. It was in January 1999. Sergio Vieira de Mello, the charismatic Under-Secretary-General for Humanitarian Affairs at the United Nations, was giving his first speech to the Security Council on the Protection of Civilians in Armed Conflict. Woven into his speech were those words of Edmund Burke. A true humanitarian, Vieira de Mello spoke with passion for people. He was calling for ethics and compliance with international law as he pled for action.

I sat right behind Vieira de Mello in the Security Council Chamber. Working for the United Nations Office for the Coordination of Humanitarian Affairs (OCHA), I had been listening to his style and words since assuming my duties a few months previously. I noticed early on that ethics were at the center of his humanitarian mission. So when asked to draft his first speech to the Security Council, I was more than delighted. I was deeply inspired.

As I watched Vieira de Mello deliver his speech, I saw those values and ethics unfold in a passionate plea for action before the Council members. He inspired diplomats and bureaucrats, as he concluded by paraphrasing Vaclav Havel, "We must not be afraid of dreaming 'the impossible' if we want 'the impossible' to become a reality."[73]

The Security Council was mesmerized. The atmosphere was elevating. Delegates began to take the floor in an earnest and positive spirit, some venturing beyond their prepared remarks, one quoting Cervantes. The then UN Secretary-General, Kofi Annan, called and congratulated Vieira de Mello after the session. His unprecedented briefing to the Security Council had triggered something different, something new. His leadership had just made the seemingly impossible possible. For a brief moment, *realpolitik* was lost, as Council members sought only to be inspired by Vieira de Mello.

An hour later, Vieira de Mello gathered a few of us in his team in his office on the 36th floor in the UN Secretariat, the high rise between the East River and First Avenue. We congregated on the couches around his coffee table and reflected on the briefing. He was upbeat and his excitement was palpable as he asked us what had brought about such rousing energy during his briefing. We tried to grasp the reasons and find explanations. I could feel an answer inside me on the tip of my tongue, but at that point did not feel comfortable enough to express it. As I did not want to risk looking like a fool. I kept my unconventional thoughts to myself.

Inside though, I felt we had just experienced a glimpse of something profound set in motion - a *presque-vue* of something incredible waiting to be discovered. Silently, I asked myself how we could sustain the experience of such a treasured moment: of ethical politics coming alive.

*

Sixteen years have gone by since that January day in 1999, and nearly twenty-seven years have passed since I first joined the United Nations and I have not ceased pondering how we can sustain the glimpse. "Try not to be a man of success, but rather a man of values,"[74] a voice awakes me from my contemplation. It is Einstein opening the discussion. He leans to rest on the arm of his seat, while his hand cradles an unlit pipe.

I can relate. My mother always told me, when I was growing up; "First look to serve, then the rest will follow." With this guidance, I came to realize that all great leadership and achievements for humankind have been driven by values from where success has ensued. The reverse seldom rings true. Success, in itself, is not virtue. Nor can values without action be considered a success.

"The greatest virtues are those which are most useful to other persons,"[75] Aristotle reaffirms from his seat in the middle row. I see heads nodding. As the discussion descends deeper, we are hit by a momentary urge for self inquiry. Indeed, are we success driven or value driven?

We know our values, but how do we define success? We have spent decades drafting conventions and analyzing the letter of the law. We have articulated and documented a great value system. But to what extent and degree have we brought it to life? As we prod through these questions, George Bernard Shaw's earlier statement rings in the back of my mind: *Only on paper has humanity yet achieved glory...*

Our legal frameworks cannot be considered a success until they transform people's lives. The greatest challenge we face today is not the lack of laws, but rather the ability to translate laws into action. We are faced with a massive 'compliance gap,' and we seem unable to close it.

"The realities of the world are a constant reminder that global action and collective efforts are now needed more than ever," says Jan Eliasson, the charismatic Deputy Secretary-General of the United Nations, "I think we are a reflection of the world as it is and not as we want it to be – but we have to bridge that gap, make sure we want the world to become more of what we want it to be."[76] Eliasson knows well the gap that needs to be closed between our vision and mission, having served as the Under-Secretary-General of the Department for Humanitarian Affairs, the President of the General Assembly, as well as the Foreign Minister of Sweden.

Once more, silence overtakes us. As disparity deepens, as the gap widens, we are approaching a dangerous, perhaps irreversible, state of the world.

As we ponder on the abyss, Aristotle returns to the debate. This time he stands and makes a short, but well chosen comment, pointing at the threat, "At his best, man is the noblest of all animals; separated from law and justice he is the worst."[77]

He reminds us of the world as it is today.

We cannot claim that we are at our best. By all accounts, we are not there as a human family. We are, in fact, drifting further away from law and justice. In the void, many millions of cries go unheard. From the refugee camps of Khan Younis and Yarmuk to the displaced persons' camps in El Geneina and Goma, and all those drifting in rubber boats on the Mediterranean, people want to know how our conventions translate into their lives in their darkest hours. They want to know why we don't heed their calls. They demand an answer. We are compelled to find it. Where did we go wrong?

As if reading our minds, Desmond Tutu rises from his chair in the front row and turns around, "Freedom and liberty lose out by default because good people are not vigilant,"[78] he states factually before retreating to his seat.

Einstein leans in the direction of Tutu and adds, "In matters of truth and justice, there is no difference between large and small problems, for issues concerning the treatment of people are all the same."[79]

The pieces converge before us. Combined, their remarks remind us that we need vigilance to close the chasm between the law and reality. Vigilance means constant remembrance of law and justice, in situations big or small. Failing to acknowledge justice for one person will soon become a failure to acknowledge justice for millions. Humanity lost.

"We fought injustice wherever we found it, no matter how large, or how small, and we fought injustice to preserve our own humanity,"[80] recalls Nelson Mandela in a thoughtful reflection on his own experience on Robben Island.

Their words sink in. We sit and contemplate quietly. It is when we fail to be vigilant to law and justice that we begin to spiral downwards. Each time we let our attention slip from safeguarding these imperatives, we further the distance. One seemingly isolated or small decision void of vigilance is another step down in the abyss, another step further away from our humanity. Many such small decisions eventually shape the world.

Watching the debate unfold, I recall my first decade in United Nations service in the 1990s. The Cold War had come to an end. We spoke of a dialogue between civilizations. In 1993, the Vienna Conference for Human Rights convened, declaring all human rights indivisible. No longer would the East claim respect for socioeconomic rights at the cost of civil and political rights, nor would the West pride itself with the latter, while ignoring the former.

In a related development, the idea of "human security" was brought into United Nations Security Council deliberations to balance the notion of "national security." There was a growing consensus that people's security and protection was essential to maintain international [and regional] peace and security.

Then, almost as if to show that words and conferences alone are not enough, the world was stunned by the genocide in Rwanda in 1994 and the crimes against humanity in Srebenica in Bosnia in 1995. We were forced to dive deeper into our consciousness. Kofi Annan launched the concept of "humanitarian intervention." No longer could Member States hide behind "sovereignty" to justify gross violations of international law.

The theme of Protection of Civilians emerged on the agenda, bringing much inspiration to our work. Over lunches, coffee and behind closed door consultations, we shaped this vision together with diplomats on the Security Council. This was followed by the Responsibility to Protect (R2P), while rights-based approaches mushroomed across the international aid system. As vigilance rose, each step of progressive and individual contribution laid another building block for a shift in our collective thoughts, speech and action. Hope emerged once more. The United Nations was returning to its essence.

This decade of enlightenment, however, came to an abrupt end in 2001 with the atrocious terror attack on the World Trade Center in New York City. As an immediate reaction, national security was placed at the forefront swallowing all other efforts in one single bite. Military and security expertise appeared in international aid conferences and seminars, championing security and sweeping aside justice. Decisions were taken on a daily basis, large or small, to venture further into the domain of security and further away from justice. The United Nations was under pressure to turn into an advocate for national security at the costs of human security, and thus international security. We were all losing the essence.

In this environment, in the mid 2000s, I led the establishment of the United Nations Development Programme's (UNDP) Global Rule of Law Programme in Crisis Countries. I was working for the Bureau for Crisis Prevention and Recovery, led ably by several admirable UN officials over the years, with whom I had the privilege to work: Omar Bakhet, Julia Taft, Kathleen Cravero and Jordan Ryan. There was an acute need to shift perceptions from a growing focus on national security to one that recognizes justice and *human* security as the foundational pillars for the rule of law. The hope of the 1990s was fading slowly. With this in mind, my legal team and I set out to shape the global agenda towards the rule of law. Together with lawyer colleagues across the UN system, we jointly advocated for a return of justice to the international aid discourse. In meeting after meeting in the Hague, Brussels, London, Paris and Washington DC, we argued for the essence of the rule of law. Eventually, we progressed in changing the narrative and priorities among some actors. But the fact remains to this day: national security constitutes the norm, and is frequently used as a cover for violations of international law.

"By declaring a 'war on terror' after September 11, we set the wrong agenda for the world.... when you wage war, you inevitably create innocent victims,"[81] George Soros, the self-made business magnate, observes. His organization, Open Society, spends $500 million annually to advance freedom and human rights.

Definitely, national security can never be a legitimate justification for violating peoples' most fundamental human rights, such as the freedom from torture, equality irrespective of race, ethnicity, gender or religion, the right to due process or equality before the law. The denial of *human* security always leads to conflict, hence the loss of our humanity. At the root lies the loss of vigilance. Expediency and partisanship lead to selectivity and a discriminatory application of international law. This in turn leads to impunity and compromise of the rule of law. The final result is injustice, violence, and human suffering. This vicious circle has no end. It is the logic of a wrong agenda; its cause and effect.

An uncompromising woman stands up whom I recognize as Nekibe Kelmendi. Her husband, a prominent human rights lawyer, and their two sons were executed at point blank range during the war in Kosovo 1999. She will never forget the violent knocks on the door, or the armed men who took her husband and sons away from their home in Pristina to be summarily executed on a dark night by the side of the road in Kosovo.

"I called his cell phone all night. No answer. At dawn, an automated woman's voice responded. His cell phone line had been cut off. Then, I knew," Nekibe Kelmendi told me, her eyes inconsolable.

I met her deceased husband, Bajram Kelmendi, during my time in the Balkans in the mid-1990s when, as a human rights lawyer in my early thirties, I worked for the United Nations High Commissioner for Refugees (UNHCR). I was inspired by the clarity and commitment that epitomized Bajram Kelmendi, a person of great moral courage. He headed the Council for the Defense of Human Rights and Freedoms in Kosovo, as his people suffered from systematic discrimination.

Twelve years later, in 2008, I was back in Kosovo on a mission and met with his widow in her office in Pristina. Equally admirable, she possessed the rare combination of both courage and modesty. Nekibe Kelmendi had just been appointed the Minister for Justice. As she recollected the painful events that no human deserves, I was inspired by her indomitable will and her extraordinary strength.

"We must be unbiased and deliver justice regardless of race, ethnicity or gender, so to protect universal values," says Nekibe Kelmendi as she takes the floor now and speaks of very real situations in which she, herself, was once at the receiving end. For a person with a deep sense of justice, there is no justification for selectivity or impunity. Hers is not a sentimental wish, but a steadfast principle. She experienced unspeakable injustice. The kind of injustice that either destroys you or motivates you: to succumb or survive. She chose the latter.

"Seeing her so motivated to get out of bed and deal with all the tough issues, given her background ... if she can do it, nothing can stop us!" a colleague told me. After her personal tragedy Nekibe Kelmendi dedicated her life to justice for others. She had suffered an irreversible tragedy and justice would never be hers. Yet, she kept moving for others.

"There can be no compromise on the fundamental principles of the rule of law. The respect for human rights is divine," Nekibe Kelmendi concludes, over a coffee in her office in Pristina, recounting the founding values of the United Nations. Her enlightening remarks return us to the core and point us at the path.

"If we are to go forward, we must go back and rediscover those precious values,"[82] Martin Luther King, Jr. stands in the Chamber and calls for an attitudinal shift, his arms leaning against the table, his head upright. There is not a soul in the Chamber ready to contest his passionate appeal.

But, how do we return to those values? Is it sufficient to articulate them in man-made laws? Or do we need something deeper, something more powerful that also invokes our vigilance? Do we need something that sets our virtues in motion, and pays instant attention to justice to preserve our humanity, to paraphrase Mandela?

Immanuel Kant signals a request to speak. He slowly bends forward, his eyes gazing upwards, "Two things fill my mind with ever new and increasing admiration and awe, the more often and steadily I reflect upon them: the starry heavens above me and the moral law within me."[83]

Kant's poetical words hold the key to a more profound response to our questions. It is the moral law within that makes us humane. It is the starry heavens above us that gives us strength to sustain it. The moral law within compels us to stand up for universal values. It instinctively guides us to distinguish between right and wrong against the yardstick of international law. And, it is vigilance to this moral law within that moves us to action.

Stephane Hessel, who served as a United Nations diplomat and ambassador overseeing the drafting of the Universal Declaration of Human Rights nods at Kant and rises to speak:

"If you want to be a real human being - a real woman, a real man - you cannot tolerate things which put you to indignation, to outrage. You must stand up. The worst possible outlook is indifference that says, "I can't do anything about it; I'll just get by." Behaving like that deprives you of one of the essentials of being human: the capacity and the freedom to feel outraged. That freedom is indispensable, as is the political involvement that goes with it."[84]

Hessel, the auther of *Indignez - Vous* (Time for Outrage) retreats to his seat. His impassioned call serves as a stark reminder of Gandhi's words: *the greatness of humanity is not to be human, but to be humane.*

"What would induce anyone, at this stage, to hold on to power only to be remembered for their inability to take action when it was urgent and necessary to do so?" Pope Francis asks, as he appears from the midst of the crowded Council Chamber.

He continues, "Human dignity is the same for all human beings: when I trample on the dignity of others, I trample on my own." Pope Frances concludes his statement. The progressive and non-dogmatic Argentinian pope transcends the limitations of both doctrine and politics in ways that inspire millions. Known for possessing the rare combination of both humility and bold courage, he is not afraid to ask the questions of our time.

Standing before any injustice, we are free to choose our response in any given moment. We also have a responsibility to make the right choice. When we lose our inherent capacity to be vigilant before injustice, large or small, we become the good individual who inadvertently fuels injustice in the world, or the good individual who does nothing to protect others from its toxins.

"Every person on earth plays a central role in the history of the world, either by acting or by silencing,"[85] says Paulo Coelho with the knowing look of someone who sought an answer and found it. In a single sentence, the world renowned Brazilian novelist reminds us of the interdependence between ourselves and the world, and the role we play in the larger scheme of things.

Frederick Douglass glances at Coelho and connects straightaway. He nods in agreement and opens his palms, as he speaks, "Inaction is followed by stagnation. Stagnation is followed by pestilence and pestilence is followed by death,"[86] says the African-American slave who freed himself and went on to lead the abolition movement in the United States.

They help us uncover the answer. Silence is both inaction and denial in the face of injustice. When we choose not to speak, or not to act, under the disguise of an ill defined notion of "diplomacy," allegiance or political neutrality,[87] we become that silent bystander. As the speakers align, we ask ourselves whether these notions are consistent with our vision and mission, our values and sense for justice.

"Justice consists not in being neutral between right and wrong, but in finding the right and upholding it wherever found against the wrong,"[88] Theodore Roosevelt, the legendary US President, and Nobel Peace Prize Laureate, remarks with a clear voice that sounds across the Chamber.

Behind me I overhear subtle whispers. Someone is arguing with his neighbor that there is no such thing as "right" or "wrong," but all is meant to be and all serves a purpose. This may be so, I think to myself. Life inevitably encompasses both light and darkness. Yet, the dialectic of life is not the end, but the means. We are not here simply to be human. We are here to *become humane*. In a world striving for peaceful and just coexistence, international law determines right and wrong. It offers a road map that distinguishes between cruelty and compassion; between inhumanity and humanity.

"It is a matter of taking the side of the weak against the strong, something the best people have always done," [89] Harriet Beecher Stowe reiterates Roosevelt's words. The antislavery campaigner during the Civil War in the United States lends her wisdom, and untangles intellectual reasoning into the basic tenats of our humanity.

The mood of expectation and inspiration rises, as the speakers come forward. With a hint of growing emotion, Martin Luther King, Jr. encapsulates their comments in a crystal clear illustration, "Cowardice asks 'Is it safe? Expedience asks: 'is it politic'? Vanity asks: Is it popular"? But, conscience asks 'is it right'?" Luther King, Jr. pauses for a moment before resuming, his voice loud and clear, "The ultimate measure of a man is not where he stands in moments of comfort and convenience, but where he stands at times of challenge and controversy."[90]

The debate transitions to silence as we process the unflinching statements of those who sided with our shared humanity.

However, the silence does not last long. The subject matter has clearly spurred strong sentiments shared by many of the participants. Another steady voice now speaks from the top rows of seats, "You can resolve to live your life with integrity. Let your credo be this: Let the lie come into the world, let it even triumph. But not through me." [91]

We all turn and see the Russian writer, and Nobel Literature Laureate, Aleksandr Solzhenitsyn. Once called "The Conscience of the 21st Century," Solzhenitsyn spent nearly ten years in the Gulag for exercising his freedom of conscience. His words urge others to come forward. Vigor wafts across the Chamber, like an early morning mist. We wake up and come alive.

"What is a rebel? Someone who says 'no.'" "Every act of rebellion expresses nostalgia for innocence and an appeal to the essence of being"[92] Albert Camus points out, calmly, remaining in his chair. The remark by the French Nobel Prize Laureate in Literature sends a thrill of excitement up our spines. He reminds us of the preamble of the Universal Declaration of Human Rights:

> *"Whereas it is essential, if man is not to be compelled to have recourse, as a last resort to rebellion against tyranny and oppression, that human rights should be protected by the rule of law.../..."*

Enthused by the debate, we piece together the remarks of the sages: the moral law within and the starry heaven above us inspire nonviolent rebellion for justice and humanity. It is so because these imperatives are inherent in human nature. Enshrined in the Universal Declaration for Human Rights, these are, as Nkebe Kelmendi noted, our divine birthrights.

Yet, as the speakers who stand before us today demonstrate by their own living examples, vigilance for justice and humanity is a herculean challenge. It demands constant awareness of the moral law within. Even more, it expects a depth of awareness that sparks action. Then, the moral dilemma creeps up to us: vigilance acted upon triggers consequences and even sacrifices, often very painful ones.

Yet, in the long run is it not more tormenting to give up one's integrity and let go of one's humanity?

As we try to conceal our moral predicaments Gandhi observes us and responds to our silent questions: "A 'No' uttered from the deepest conviction is better than a 'Yes' merely uttered to please, or worse, to avoid trouble."[93] "There is a higher court than courts of justice and that is the court of conscience. It supersedes all other courts." [94]

These enlightening remarks stir our thoughts. The moral law within – our conscience - is our ultimate safeguard. In the stillness of our conscience, justice is not partial; it neither personalizes, nor politicizes. We do not judge the person, but rather the act. At the core of our humanity, we show mercy and forgiveness towards the person, but do not compromise international law. In the moment of absolute vigilance, we act on our values to protect the human family. The moral law within is that most powerful force without which we cannot close the compliance gap between the law and reality.

"It is not what a lawyer tells me I may do; but what humanity, reason, and justice tell me I ought to do,"[95] Edmund Burke interrupts our flickering thoughts as they bounce back and forth between our minds and hearts. As a lawyer, I can resonate with his statement. It mirrors my own observations from the frontlines.

One of those lies in Afghanistan, a war-torn country beyond the Hindukush Mountains. Afghanistan was my first crisis country deployment with the United Nations. Following the peace accord between Afghanistan and the USSR in 1989, and the withdrawal of Soviet troops, I arrived in Kabul in the summer of 1990. Confronted with widespread destruction, abject poverty and continued shelling of Kabul from Mu-

jaheeden positions in the surrounding mountains, I yearned to understand humanity and find answers. Traveling between government and
Mujahedeen controlled areas, I spoke with people, asked questions and
observed. I learned of Pir Sayyid Ahmed Gailani who was the leader of
the Qadiriyya Sufi Order, and an Afghan Mujahedeen commander during the Soviet-Afghanistan war in the 1980s. In contrast to the brutality
of the conflict, Pir Gailani treated Soviet prisoners of war with respect
and dignity. He ensured that they had access to books and visits by the
International Committee of the Red Cross (ICRC). Torture was prohib-
ited. In large, his treatment of prisoners of war complied with the Third
Geneva Convention of 1949. I was intrigued and questioned an Afghan
friend of mine, Hameed, who had served under Pir Gailani's command.

"Does it mean that your commander [Pir Gailani] was familiar with
international humanitarian law, the Geneva Conventions?" I asked him.
"No, he knew nothing about the Geneva Conventions," Hameed, looked
at me and smiled, pointing his index finger towards his heart, "It was his
humanity."

His response helped me understand. From my earliest days of UN
service in Afghanistan, I have seen this humanity reappear on the frontlines, time and again.

Another such frontline lay in the heart of Europe, the Balkans - a
region where borders were carved in blood in a gruesome war. In the
mid 1990s, I worked for the United Nations High Commissioner for Refugees (UNHCR) in Montenegro and Bosnia during and after the war. I interviewed thousands of refugees for protection and resettlement, each
sharing their personal story of injustice and human suffering. I negotiated with war criminals to obtain protection and gain passage for those
refugees. Amidst all the darkness, there were glimpses of humanity.

Once in northwestern Bosnia, a colleague recollected an event
that illustrates the daily reality of that war, one which had made a deep
imprint on her. Soldiers had entered the property of a family and shot
dead the husband on the staircase to their home. Standing next to him,

his wife and their son had just witnessed the summary execution when one of the soldiers turned his gun towards the son. In an instant, the mother gathered her last strength and called out, "Spare my son and I shall bring him up to forgive what you have done to his father." In a split second, the universe aligned the stars and the solar systems for this single mother about to lose her son. The soldier lowered his gun and left.

In the darkest corners of the globe, amidst unspeakable cruelty and inhumanity, I have encountered individuals with a story of conscience – the moral law awakened either their own conscience or others'. These were individuals, civilians, soldiers or armed individuals, who did something to spare the world from more toxic injustice; another violation of international law. Many of them did not know of our conventions, but they were touched by their conscience amidst adversity and moral dilemmas. They testify to a timeless truth: if we are to achieve compliance with international law, we have to touch the conscience of humanity, the moral law within, both in the perpetrators committing the crimes and in ourselves committed to upholding international law. To distill the gist of Kant's famous lines, besides the law, we also need to draw upon what lies within us and above us.

"Deep down, below the surface of the average man's conscience, he hears a voice whispering, 'There is something not right,' no matter how much his rightness is supported by public opinion or moral code,"[96] Carl Jung, the world renowned Swiss psychoanalyst, rises and speaks. His words validate those of Immanuel Kant and Hameed, alike.

Indeed, the humanitarians, scientists, philosophers, artists, politicians, and the stoical people in war gave me the answers. Far beyond the lecture halls of our law faculties and legal conferences, they showed me that alone the law cannot save the world. We can only close the gap between the law and reality once we integrate the essence of the law into our being, and the essence of our being into action.

From there emerges a powerful force of humanity, or as Solzhenitsyn exclaims aloud in closing, "A society which is based on the letter of the law and never reaches any higher is taking very scarce advantage of the high level of human possibilities."[97]

*

As the discussion on this agenda item draws to an end, my mind returns to a briefing before the Security Council in 1999. Sergio Vieira de Mello had appealed to the essence. He had ignited a light within all sitting around the horseshoe table.  On that January day, the moral law within had been awakened in a precious moment of inspiration.

From then on I knew that it was indeed possible to lift our hearts to a new level of humanity even within a large bureaucracy and its political chambers, amongst diplomats and political actors.

We had seen a glimpse of human possibility.
But how do we sustain that glimpse? For only in so doing shall we more vigorously narrow the distance between ourselves and our universal vision.  Only then shall we close the 'compliance-gap' *between the world as it is and the world as we would like it to be*, to paraphrase Eliasson.

Today, I know for certain that, something more is needed to attain this human possibility. And I believe that 'something more' is the human potential for moral progress.

"The first principle of value that we need to rediscover is this: that all reality hinges on moral foundations," Martin Luther King, Jr remarks and continues, "In other words, that this is a moral universe, and that there are moral laws of the universe just as abiding as the physical laws."[98]

We digest Luther King, Jr's words, which bear a strong resemblance to those of the previous speakers. We see faces across the Chamber who have spoken to us about the essence of justice and humanity. We connect the dots between laws and values. To close the gap between the law and reality, we also need to close the gap between our values and our actions - inside ourselves. This is moral progress.

"These virtues are formed in man by his doing the actions…," Aristotle returns to the debate once more and concludes the discussion. Known for his ability to see the universality in all things, he lends insights to the remarks made, pointing at Ambassador Mackenzie's earlier statement, which suggested that "everyone must start with themselves."

In doing so, Aristotle unveils the path towards progress: "The good of man is a working of the soul in the way of excellence in a complete life."[99]

# Agenda Item 4
# Courage and Conviction:
# Dare Something Worthy

*"I am not afraid... I was born to do this,"*

*Jeanne D'Arc*

Row upon row of different colored leather seats are filled with men and women of greatness from the past and present, alongside all of us who are inspired by them. "What a mind-blowing occasion," someone behind me whispers, certain that we all share the same sense of exhilaration. Once more, the sound of the gavel striking signals the start of a new agenda item, demanding our attention. The President calls for Mahatma Gandhi to start the next agenda item.

"Man becomes great exactly in the degree in which he works for the welfare of his fellow-men," [100] Gandhi picks up from where Aristotle has left off. Gandhi's opening statement is followed rapidly by another.

"Safeguarding the rights of others is the most noble and beautiful end of a human being,[101]" Khalil Gibran, the Lebanese author and poet, rises and matches Gandhi's words.

Their introductory remarks soar across the Chamber. They have spoken to the *completeness* of life. Can there be a grander standard of achievement for anyone seeking fulfillment or a world aspiring to civilization? The founders of the United Nations did not think so. They enshrined those standards in the United Nations Charter and the Universal

Declaration of Human Rights on the assumption that we - seven billion people - would strive to be free from fear.

"In a political context of the utmost significance, freedom from fear recognizes a human right which, in a broad sense, may be said to sum up the whole philosophy of human rights,"[102] Dag Hammarskjold leans forward and reaffirms the premise for our standards of achievement. He reminds us that human rights are part of the political context - a context that also requires freedom from fear.

Though the Security Council lacks windows to the outside world, the wisdom of the speakers illuminates the Chamber. They remind us that fear cannot sustain the glimpse. Rather, it is fear that maintains the gap between the law and reality; between the conscience of humanity and the world as it is.

A fearless advocate for humanism, Bertrand Russell stands up in the gallery. As he announces his intention to speak, our heads turn. A grin appears on Russell's face. In the spirit of his own life, Russell ties the statements together, "Neither a man nor a crowd nor a nation can be trusted to act humanely or to think sanely under the influence of a great fear."[103] His remark shakes us awake from our slumber. We realize the impact that fear has on our very being.

Fear is both the spiky fence of cruelty and the grey wall of indifference that separates "we" from "them." Fear is on our side of the fence. Courage is on theirs. Fear advises "it may harm my career," or "it is too risky." Fear does not ask "is it right?" It looks at interests rather than beliefs, so *words lose their meaning*, to paraphrase Confucius' earlier remarks. Fear searches for security outside rather than for safety within. It cannot bear to sacrifice itself, either for our values, or for the future of our children.

"The future does not belong to those who are content with today, apathetic toward common problems and their fellow man alike, timid and fearful in the face of bold projects and new ideas," Robert

Kennedy steps forward and lends his support to the debate. He points at the hundreds of participants who have traveled from afar, as he concludes, "Rather, it will belong to those who can blend passion, reason and courage in a personal commitment to ideals."[104] He offers another clue to the completeness of life, and perhaps also the merits of a twenty-first century leader.

We are reminded, once more, of yet another universal experience. From my years in countries of conflict, amongst people who have suffered unspeakable atrocities and choking oppression, but who survived, all have one thing in common: they conquered their fears for the sake of justice and humanity. Through courageous and conscientious choices they pushed through the fence separating "we" from "them," even at the cost of life itself.

I search the records of my memory and recall one such example. It played out in the spring of 1999 amidst the mass expulsion of the Kosovars. Watching from afar in the safe confines of my New York office, I had just learned of the execution of the high-profile human rights lawyer, Bajram Kelmendi and his two sons. As the tragic news reached me, my mind kept probing questions about my own courage and meaning in life. Who was I? Was I really the human rights lawyer I had aspired to become? While wrestling with my internal discomfort inside the comfort zone, I heard of another execution which had taken place in Kosovo.

On this May day in 1999, an unsung hero, whom I had met during my time in the Balkans, the prominent Kosovar politician, Fehmi Agani, and his family, set out to flee besieged Kosovo. The population was incommunicado and Agani sought to cross the border to tell the world of the war crimes then being committed. As he risked the same fate as Kelmendi he disguised himself in a long black coat and brown scarf wrapped around his head, anonymously joining the columns of fleeing Kosovars.

After shuffling into train compartments, thousands endured the journey hoping to cross into safety in Macedonia. But just before the border, the train came to a sudden halt. Soldiers entered the cars, ordering all passengers to step off. They were then lined up in a field. A handful of soldiers walked along the line selecting young men for execution. Moments before, Agani had been a potential target. Now, he was a bystander. As terrified young men were selected, Agani stepped out of the crowd and tossed aside his disguise. He was sacrificing himself.

Agani's presence reverberated through the air. He was a high-ranking political figure, the deputy to President Ibrahim Rugova, who was then being held hostage in Belgrade. Given his political visibility, Agani could neither be a witness, nor could he be executed without orders from the highest levels. The confused soldiers let the young men go and instead captured Agani. Following communication with their superiors, they placed him on a bus back to Pristina. At the outskirts of Pristina, police officers entered the bus and apprehended him. A few days later, Agani was found dead with three bullets in his body.

"They whose heart is firm, and whose conscience approves their conduct, will pursue their principles unto death,"[105] Leonardo da Vinci points out quietly, as we process the fate of Agani and those of his ilk. Theirs is a daily struggle to conquer the fear of death. For them, the alternative is a life without values and principles, which is also a form of death.

"You can chain me, you can torture me, you can even destroy this body, but you will never imprison my mind,"[106] Gandhi says, illustrating the experience of profoundly felt courage.

Gandhi's testimony is quickly reiterated by Khalil Gibran, who shares a similar disposition to courage, "You may chain my hands, you may shackle my feet; you may even throw me into a dark prison; but you shall not enslave my thinking, because it is free!"[107]

The Chamber retreats into self reflection. As we contemplate the emotional strength and profound depth of their statements, we know that their feelings are shared by millions living in the cold and harsh reality of man's inhumanity to man.  Here, in the safe confines of our carpeted and window less chamber, how do we relate to them?

*

Dare something worthy - *Aude aliquid dignum*. That which is genuinely worthy begets an extraordinary power of passion and grace: passion to move forward in the face of obstacles and controversy until grace descends and renders it possible, or *Baraka* as they say in Arabic, Hebrew, Swahili, Urdu, Turkish and Persian.

In a world of so much suffering, one is bound to ask whether there is anything that connects us in a more worthy cause than the United Nations. In fact, most of us will not contest values that protect and treat all human beings equally and optimally. But what holds us back from materializing those values, individually and collectively?

We cannot blame it on bureaucracy or Member States. For, we are those. We operate the bureaucracy, we shape the structures, and we - not "them" and "us" - are the United Nations. Rather, the question for the twenty-first century is whether we, all of us - as human beings and nations - are connected and fit for a purpose?
Do we dare?

"Few men are willing to brave the disapproval of their fellows, the censure of their colleagues, the wrath of their society. Moral courage is a rarer commodity than bravery in battle or great intelligence. Yet it is one essential, vital quality for those who seek to change a world which yields most painfully to change,"[108] Robert Kennedy's mighty statement echoes across the Chamber. He has just touched upon the real impediments that stand before us daily: the stumbling blocks are ultimately our own. We build those barriers inside ourselves and hence, outside.

The Chamber pauses for reflection. We ask ourselves how we can transcend the walls we build within, so we can raze those we build without? We have choices to make. Without moral courage to act in the face of violent danger and political obstacles, what is left as a worthwhile offering to the millions sustained only by moral courage in their dark prison cells, cramped refugee camps, or in the ruin of their communities?

"The truth," exclaims Harriet Beecher Stowe, "is the kindest thing we can give people in the end."[109]

*

The fear that fails to speak the truth, or simply the plain fear to fail, is the same fear that weakens our power to inspire and mold consensus around our universal values.

"There is only one thing that makes a dream impossible to achieve: the fear of failure,[110]" Paolo Coelho states, crossing his arms and gazing ahead. He captures the emotion that lies at the core of a vision unattained: fear of failure compromises our commitment and makes us settle for the lowest common denominator.

"Only those who dare to fail greatly can ever achieve greatly."[111] Robert Kennedy continues the theme, running his fingers through his hair. He takes a breath as if gearing up, and says, "Each time a man stands up for an ideal, or acts to improve the lot of others, or strikes out against injustice, he sends forth a tiny ripple of hope, and those ripples build a current which can sweep down the mightiest walls of oppression and resistance."[112]

Once more, we are thrown back into quiet deliberation. Hard choices are to be made. Daring to achieve means speaking truth to power, and it coexists with consequences. In fact, the two are positively inseparable and interdependent. Without consequences, one cannot cultivate strength and moral muscle to strike out against injustice and inspire a ripple effect of hope. Thus, the consequences are not the real stumbling points. Rather, they are building blocks for attaining courage towards moral progress and completeness.

"Let your courage rise with danger,"[113] Nelson Mandela says, as a smile spreads across his face. Behind him, Anaïs Nin, the Cuban-French poet, taps his shoulder and beams in agreement. "Life shrinks or expands in proportion to one's courage,"[114] she summarizes.

We connect. It is fear that holds us back and confines us to the incompleteness of life. Conversely, courage paves the way for excellence in a complete life. Sensing our rising awareness, another poet comes forward. It is Hafiz, the Persian mystic. He looks across the auditorium and nods in a show of consent.

"Fear is the cheapest room in the house. I would like to see you living in better conditions."[115] He turns towards the horseshoe table, raising his voice. "Now is the time to know that all you do is sacred. Now is the time for you to deeply compute the impossibility that there is anything but grace.[116] Let's get loose with compassion."[117]

An awkward silence sets in. Some appear uncomfortable with Hafiz's seemingly sentimental urging. They look down. Others gaze at him with respect. They know his value and the sincerity of his call. Compassion is the feeling of the brave and profound.

As the amicable exchange between visionary politicians and passionate artists continues, Desmond Tutu takes the floor and reinforces Hafiz's statement, "Frequently, people think compassion and love are merely sentimental. No! They are very demanding. If you are going to be compassionate, be prepared for action."[118] Tutu walks across the floor to give weight to his statement. His challenge throws us into greater probing of the broader meaning of compassion.

Compassion means understanding without accepting. "We are more effective when we apply compassion to establish justice rather than just resorting to confrontation," says John Pace, a staunch human rights lawyer, under whose leadership I first served at the United Nations then Center for Human Rights in 1988. In a long career with the UN, Pace faced many obstacles in his commitment to human rights, but always survived and indeed thrived. Now seventy-five and retired he nonetheless continues his mission for those on the other side of the fence. This is compassion.

Where there is compassion, there is courage. The two form the sturdy foundation for our humanity. One cannot do without the other. Where there is compassion for mistakes, there is also courage to learn from our failures and to do things right.

"Once we realize that imperfect understanding is the human condition, there is no shame in being wrong, only in failing to correct our mistakes" [119] George Soros says aloud. His words ease our self-inquiry. The quest for completeness is itself one of compassion. We may fail repeatedly, but as long as we muster courage to try once more, we are moving forward. Just as compassion understands without accepting, and gives without expecting, compassion also means the courage to forgive.

"To achieve justice in its broader sense we need to have compassion for our enemies and the wisdom to make peace with them," says José Ramos-Horta. Besides leading Timor Leste into peaceful relations with Indonesia at the national level, Ramos-Horta also made peace at the individual level, forgiving the East Timorese gunmen who tried to assassinate him in 2008. "My message to my people is please forgo violence and hatred with weapons, machetes, with arson - we only destroy each other and the country,"[120] he said when emerging from the hospital after the assassination attempt.

I look around the Chamber to gauge reactions. A question is on everyone's lips: what stands between us and the daring actions of compassion and courage? What is the barrier that prevents compassion and courage from merging into a powerful force to attain human potential, as envisioned in 1945?

This is the question of our times and the one whose answer we so urgently need to bring to light.

Fear stands in between. It is the fear to fail, the fear to lose power, and the fear of freedom that removes our humanity. This is what the 'will to power' has done to us. It drives us towards cowardice rather than courage, and steers us towards callousness rather than compassion. The consequences are severe and have brought us to where we are today.

"It is when we all play safe that we create a world of utmost insecurity," Hammarskjold takes the floor and repeats his earlier statement. He gathers his thoughts for a moment, and then expands, "It is when we all play safe that fatality will lead us to our doom. It is in the "dark shade of courage" alone that the spell can be broken."[121]

We listen. We understand. But, we find it hard to break the spell. Even when we choose to struggle with our fears in times of adversity, we often fall short of going the whole way. We may set out to achieve a worthy goal, but abandon it in the face of mounting obstacles. Glorious commitments tend to fade, and high-flown promises vanish bit by bit. We defer and compromise, breeding new injustices that snowball into greater obstacles for future generations. In the absence of courage and compassion, incompleteness becomes omnipresent.

There is an eerie feeling in the air as the Chamber digests these words. The debate is rough and tough. Breaking the spell is no routine matter. Every dent brings discomfort. "Be prepared for action," as Tutu said. Indeed, the search for moral courage is a struggle.

"Let me give you a word of the philosophy of reform," Frederick Douglass stands and offers his advice born of personal experience. "If there is no struggle there is no progress. Those who profess to favor freedom, and yet depreciate agitation, are men who want crops without plowing up the ground. They want rain without thunder and lightning. They want the ocean without the awful roar of its many waters." [122]

His statement jolts our thoughts. We stop for a moment, shredding the garments of fear, and remind ourselves of the numerous times we have urged caution in the face of human suffering. We want to awaken the world to our vision, but we don't want to question the convenience of *realpolitik*. We want justice with selectivity. We want peace without sacrifice. We want rain without thunder.

Yet, we now realize that, if we gather the courage to break the spell, there might actually be something good which comes from the jolt and the struggle.

Sensing our hesitancy to break the spell, Simone de Beauvoir, the French author and philosopher, emerges from the audience. True to character, she speaks with conviction, "Defending truth is not something one does out of a sense of duty or to allay guilt complexes, but is a reward in itself."[123] She pauses and looks around to measure the temperature in the Chamber, before she concludes with a promise, "I tore myself away from the safe comfort of certainties through my love for truth – and truth rewarded me."[124] She takes a deep breath and declares: "I wish that every human life be pure transparent freedom."[125]

*Aude aliquid dignum!*

From a distance, I see Rosa Parks stand, her hair tied elegantly in a knot. She is a physically short woman at 5'3" but her stature was tall enough to change the course of history. Parks smiles as she addresses the Council, "You must never be fearful about what you are doing when it is right. I have learned over the years that when one's mind is made up, this diminishes fear; knowing what must be done does away with fear. I was tired of giving in." By finally refusing to give up her seat in a segregated bus, she sparked the Civil Rights Movement in the United States. "Stand for something or you will fall for anything."[126]

The discussion inspires the Chamber, and we need this inspiration. The universal values of the United Nations were delivered on the heels of the struggles wrought upon us by WWII. It was a time of moral courage and compassion. The United Nations was founded on the premise that we should free ourselves and others from fear and move in determination "in larger freedom." Amidst this enlightened era of progress in modern history, every individual took personal responsibility for his or her fears to purse a collective vision.

One of them, Eleanor Roosevelt, steps forward and shares the story of overcoming her fears, "My greatest fear has always been that I would be afraid - afraid physically or mentally or morally and allow myself to be influenced by fear instead of by my honest convictions."[127] Roosevelt does not shy away from revealing her own stumbling blocks, which she was determined to raze to the ground.

Her candid confession is followed by Dag Hammarskjold's, who now takes the floor. Thoughtfully, he describes his experience, "I inherited a belief that no life was more satisfactory than one of selfless service to your country – or humanity. This service required a sacrifice of all personal interests, but likewise the courage to stand up unflinchingly for your convictions."[128] His voice rises: "Never 'for the sake of peace and quiet' deny your own experience and convictions."[129] His powerful words have spurred many to serve with conviction.

I look to Omar Bakhet next to me. He is one of those personalities whose convictions drove his work in the modern era of the United Nations. A retired senior UN official, whom I have known since the early 1990s, Bakhet's whole life is a story of conquering fears. A former child soldier in the Eritrean rebel movement, Bakhet arrived as a refugee in Sweden in the 1970s. He completed his studies in Economics at Lunds University and then joined the United Nations. His background and triumph over fear in extraordinary circumstances made him a strong asset for the world body. Bakhet spent twenty-five years serving refugees around the globe, and survivors of the genocide in Rwanda, in the most compassionate and daring ways. Never, for the sake of peace and quiet, did he deny his own convictions.

While leading the UN system in post genocide Rwanda, Bakhet looked across the border into neighboring Zaire where 1.2 million Rwandan Hutus (refugees and "genocidaires") were targeted by Congolese rebels allied with President Kabila. Even the thought of addressing this problem would not be entertained by most of us, Bakhet, however, pursued what he believed to be right in matching our vision and mission. He circumvented organizational rules to save people's lives. Driving into the darkness, he crossed the border into Zaire without permission from above, and through extraordinary skills, negotiated a deal with rebel leader Kabila, which involved giving him a satellite phone. In return, Hutu refugees could return to Rwanda and the reconciliation process could begin.

"The UN is not about us, the UN is about the people we serve," Bakhet says, "If we fear, we cannot bring about change; we cannot end suffering during the carnage of war, nor can we support reconciliation for people and nations to heal in its aftermath."

Those who have spoken today have all passed the message. It is now abundantly clear: the force that transforms fear into courage is a deeply felt conviction. Conviction is a sense of personal responsibility to do what is right from an infinite space of universality rather than from the rigid place of nationality or individuality. *This* is the premise for our vision and mission.

I spot someone else who gives a human face to this premise. It is my friend, Sami Abdelshafi, who hails from Gaza, and works for the Carter Foundation. Sami has endured three wars over the past five years. Each time, he spends long dark nights in a chair in his living room wrestling with his fears as bombs fall around his neighborhood. When the sun rises, he counts the dead with a devastated and broken heart. An American citizen, he declined the US Consulate's offer of evacuation during the last war, the summer of 2014. "How can I leave all these people suffering behind just for my own safety?" he asked me afterwards.

Now, Sami speaks, "I always wondered why some people remain silent in the face of calamity or conflict, while others speak out. Is it because they lack conviction or they lack courage, or both? But, when conviction deepens, courage is no longer a choice. It is an overwhelming energy that forces itself into being."

We fall quiet. The time has come to listen. Sami's direct experience reminds us that conviction is a state of being that is no longer concerned with fear - not even with its own virtue of courage. Conviction grows slowly and steadily from within our conscience, step by step, until it forces its way through the confining shell, breaks it open and is unleashed in sheer determination.

"One needs to be slow to form convictions, but once formed they must be defended against the heaviest odds",[130] Gandhi notes, welcoming the direction the debate is taking. As a child, Gandhi feared the dark. From there, he went on to lead India, and also Great Britain, out of the dark age of colonization.

The debate transports me back to another place where I encountered real faces of conscience and conviction: Cambodia. The year was 1992. The United Nations Transitional Authority in Cambodia (UNTAC) was mandated to repatriate millions of Khmers, restore human rights and organize free and fair elections. I was responsible for our human rights activities in Battambang, the second largest province in Cambodia. Heading a team of United Nations Civil Police, we discovered undisclosed detention centers incarcerating political prisoners.

Deployed in the northwest of the country, far from the buzzing and crowded streets of the capital, Phnom Penh, our investigation into these detention centers in the Cambodian countryside was ridden with fear. It lasted for months and meant addressing internal resistance and, eventually, mobilizing the UN mission to act. There was fear among us. Some feared that we would rock the boat. "So what's wrong with rocking the boat?" my boss, Dennis McNamara, the Director of the Human Rights Component, countered in one of those meetings with UNTAC seniors. His fearless commitment to human rights broke the hold and jolted the collective mind of the UNTAC mission.

Yet, I too was afraid. I feared for my life at times, as we circled the muddy and unpaved roads of Battambang at night to interview witnesses and collect evidence. I felt fear as we worked under the cloud of death threats jotted down on a scrap of paper, or passed on through verbal warnings. When we finally entered the prisons after months of investigation and stood face to face with the prisoners, who had courageously acted on their conviction, I knew instantly: they were the people who were truly free and had been all along.

Because they dared something worthy, we had conquered our fears to dare something worthy too. We owed our relative courage to their absolute conviction.

As the discussion reaches its conclusion, the threads of the debate come together. The moral law within – our conscience - reflexively seeks out the companionship of courage and compassion. When the desire grows stronger, the determination firmer, conviction appears and fear dissolves.

The people on the other side of the fence often travel that path and adopt those traits. They develop resilience. And so they become our teachers. They have lost everything but their humanity and longing for justice. They bring life to our laws and conventions. It is they whose spirit pushes through the brick wall of fear and who break the siege. In the harshest conditions, in the darkest spots on the globe, they dare something worthy--daily.

More than ever, we need them in our institutions, political offices and chambers.

# Agenda Item 5
# Intelligence and Knowledge:
# Understanding the Immeasurable

*"*                                                                    *"*
*It takes something more than intelligence to act intelligently.*

*Fyodor Dostoyevsky*

The President of the Security Council returns to his seat after a brief interlude. Almost everyone else is already seated. Some glance at the agenda sheet, others text on their cell phones and a few are absorbed in their own reflections. It could be another ordinary Security Council meeting about to resume. Yet, it is anything but. The President of the Council invites Carl Jung to open the next agenda item.

Jung rises and removes his round-shaped glasses, "We should not pretend to know the world only by the intellect. The judgment of the intellect is only part of the truth,"[131] Jung eloquently extracts the essence of today's debate, "Where love rules, there is no 'will to power', and where power predominates, love is lacking. The one is the shadow of the other."[132]

As he takes his seat, the Indian poet, Rabindranath Tagore exclaims, "A mind all logic is like a knife all blade. It makes the hand bleed that uses it."[133] The Nobel Prize Laureate in Literature deftly weaves another thread into the web of more complete understanding.

Indeed, much human suffering has been inflicted by stand-alone intellect divorced from the heart, *the moral law within and the starry heavens above*, to paraphrase Immanuel Kant. How many intellectuals were amongst the Nazi Germans, whose unspeakable cruelty was made possible by highly educated lawyers, engineers, architects and doctors? Thinking human beings stopped asking moral questions, stopped feeling. Their mission was to obey authority and implement instructions in the name of nationalism – not to uphold universal values and protect human beings in the name of humanity.

The prevailing school of law in Germany at the time was *positive law* which means that whatever man made law is promulgated is valid and legitimate, and supersedes any moral law. This stands in sharp contrast to *natural law,* which laid the foundation for the United Nations. In natural law, rights are inherent in human nature, and thus cannot be legislated away. At the extreme end, oppressive societies often place positive law over natural law, and use legislation to discriminate and oppress people. The other end of the spectrum refers to good individuals with good intentions, who submit to rules and regulations inconsistent with natural law, and unintentionally contribute to suffering. Where vigilance to justice is absent, we are all at risk.

As we contemplate the fatal inconsistency between the two, General Dallaire returns to the discussion. He reflects on his time in Rwanda and the lack of response from the international community.

"More and more I see lost opportunities; more and more I see errors because of lack of intelligence or simply from miss-assessing a situation," he states, knowingly.

During the genocide in Rwanda in 1994, good individuals justified inaction by referring to mandate and rules of engagement, as adopted by the Security Council. The vision of human rights as inherent in our nature had been overtaken by manmade mandates that were not consistent with the founding principles of the United Nations.

"It's horrific because every day decisions were taken on life and death. Everyday.  Real people, real people,"[134] Dallaire repeats, as he gazes across the Chamber.

It's a penetrating gaze and it hits us. The way of dealing with this human tragedy resembled a clinically intellectual response along the lines of positive law. If the mandate or rules of engagement as adopted by the Security Council did not provide for protection of people (or intervention under Chapter VII of the UN Charter), there was no legal ground for action, some said. Even as the Genocide Convention of 1948 obliges states to intervene, it was argued that the systematic killing of a specific ethnic group did not fit the legal definition of "genocide" in the Genocide Convention. Arguments against intervening to protect people's rights were made from different angles. Narrow reasoning was detached from human suffering, distanced from the spirit of natural law and the essence of international law.

One year later, in 1995, the Rwanda experience was followed by the massacres of 8000 boys and men in Srebrenica in Bosnia. And again, the failure to respond to yet another human tragedy was rationalized. At that time, I was serving with the United Nations High Commissioner for Refugees (UNHCR) in the Balkans. As the mass executions unfolded in Srebenica in Bosnia, I was only a few kilometers away in neighboring Montenegro, wrestling with a deep sense of despair in my own helplessness. I was hit by an intense feeling of disillusionment with international leaders entrusted to chart our way forward. The logical reasoning was similar to Rwanda. There was no moral courage, no political will, to intervene in the face of cruelty and suffering. Once more, the sharp edged blade had cut us off from our conscience.

Rwanda and Srebrenica eventually brought about a candid internal probing in the United Nations, and led to a renewed resolve to find solutions to strengthen the protection of civilians in armed conflict. They haunted the international community for many years until we stumbled into new episodes of grave injustice and suffering caused by reasons of national interests unaligned with the interests of humanity. And so, never again became again and again.

"We should act when we hear the vibrations on the ground. We should not say 'never again.' Each time we say 'never again,' we have failed. We should act preventively," The UN Deputy-Secretary General, Jan Eliasson, notes, adding: "the world should learn from past mistakes and act before mass atrocities take place." [135]

The repetitive pattern of inflicting, denying or failing to act in the face of injustice and human suffering shows us that intellectual reasoning, alone, does not suffice to prevent human tragedies. While our intellect is essential to analyze, assemble and make effective use of knowledge, it cannot be separate from feelings and an inner moral compass. At its best, intellect alone is ineffective in preventing suffering. At its worst, it causes more suffering - suffering that is often justified through rationalization, sometimes known as *realpolitik*.

"It is important to reclaim for humanity the ground that has been taken from it by various arbitrarily narrow formulations of the demands of rationality,"[136] Amartya Sen speaks from his seat in the front row. Author of *The Idea of Justice and Development as Freedom* and a Nobel Prize Laureate in Economics, Sen reminds us that the stand-alone rational mind is not only a narrow one, but also one that may conflict with our humanity.

Where our universal values are at stake, something far greater and vastly more profound is required from us. Not only do we need to enlarge ourselves beyond the limitations of the mind and its encroaching clutter, we also need to rearrange our order of priorities.

"We should take care not to make the intellect our god; it has, of course, powerful muscles, but no personality,"[137] Einstein explains thoughtfully before expanding on his statement. "The intuitive mind is a sacred gift and the rational mind is a faithful servant. We have created a society that honors the servant and has forgotten the gift."[138] He pauses to allow us to process his words, and then concludes firmly, "The true sign of intelligence is not knowledge, but imagination."[139]

Silently, he returns to his chair. As I look across the Chamber, I notice that most of us are deep in thought. I entertain my own thoughts which must be going through everyone's mind at this moment. While we all agree that one should not underestimate the intellect's powerful muscle, we also know that the intellect is not all there is. It is an important human trait, but it does not necessarily make us *humane*. An exclusive use of rational reasoning risks detaching us from people reducing them to numbers, while intuition connects us to people and consequently extends our empathy. In the final analysis, feeling lies in the heart, reason lies in the head. And in the head lies the ego, which holds us hostage to fear. Our most credible muscle must therefore be our heart.

"Trust your heart rather than your head,"[140] Jean-Jacques Rousseau calls out, leaning backward in his chair and crossing his arms confidently, "The world of reality has its limits; the world of imagination is boundless."

We listen attentively to one of our foremost role-models in international affairs. Rousseau influenced political and social schools of thoughts that transformed our world far beyond himself and his own lifetime in the French Revolution which, together with the American Revolution, inspired the United Nations and the Universal Declaration of Human Rights.

From the upper row, Solzhenitsyn grins in support of Rousseau's statement, and shares his own personal experience, "Gradually it was disclosed to me that the line separating good and evil passes not through states, not between classes, nor between political parties, but through every human heart."[141]

There is an introspective atmosphere in the Chamber. Some are still hesitating to let down their guard, but their inner voice is steadily working its way towards the surface, like waves approaching the shore. When the heart speaks, other hearts listen.

"When pure sincerity forms within, it is outwardly realized in other people's hearts,"[142] Lao Tzu notes, reflecting on the logic of cause and effect.

"From the heart may it reach other hearts!"[143] Ludwig van Beethoven calls out, revealing the powerful force that brings beauty and inspiration to humanity. Beethoven, a composer grappling with deafness - the irony of a great fate - defeated all reason and rose to immortality through his refined senses and feelings. He perceived the subtle tones of glorious music inside himself. "To play without passion is inexcusable. I have never thought of writing for reputation and honor. What I have in my heart must come out: that is the reason why I compose,"[144] concludes Beethoven, who crafted his masterpiece, *Ode to Joy*, with a deep desire for serving humanity.

One of the greatest composers of all times Beethoven sheds light on how we give something back to humanity, whether in the arts, politics, science, technology, medicine or any other field of service, large or small. To serve without passion is inexcusable. Passion is not a thing of the head. It is an affair of the heart.

"Speak a new language so that the world becomes a new world, only from the heart can you touch the sky,"[145] the 13th century Persian poet, Jalalludin Rumi says, gently. One of the most advanced travelers on the journey within, the world renowned Sufi mystic returns with valuable wisdom in his luggage that must not be lost; because when the rest of us reach the destination and find the answers, it may be too late.

It takes emotional intelligence to reach the hearts of others. Emotional intelligence does not instruct. It inspires. Through empathy, it transcends the wall between "we" and "them." Through intuition, it reveals the larger picture well before the last piece is laid. It knows what needs to be done and makes the connection. We become more responsive and move faster – all highly imperative in a life or death crisis. As General Dallaire said, *Everyday. Real people, real people.* At the other end, disconnection is opportunity lost. Humanity lost.

"Does your organization have a mission statement?" the author Daniel Goleman asks in his bestselling book, *Emotional Intelligence.* If so, "Does the mission statement describe the day-to-day reality of life there?" Because, as he explains, "When there is a glaring gap between the espoused vision of an organization and the actual reality, the inevitable emotional fallout can range from self-protective cynicism to anger and even despair." For this reason, he concludes, "An emotionally intelligent organization needs to come to terms with any disparities between the values it proclaims and those it lives."[146]

We make the connection. Day-to-day reality does not always match the standards of achievement we have set for the world. We do not feel where we should be feeling. The challenge is not just to align thoughts, words and action, but to glue them with love, to put in context Jung's opening remarks. Emotional intelligence aligns us with our vision at a deeper level. It is the level that moves us to action.

"Without passion, nothing happens; without compassion, the wrong thing happens, the United Nations Deputy-Secretary General, Jan Eliasson, hits the target.

"Emotion is the chief source of all becoming conscious." Says Carl Jung as he leans towards his microphone, "There can be no transforming of darkness into light and of apathy into movement without emotion."[147]

Dr. Zuleta Angel, when calling the first General Assembly to order, must have had an inkling of this. Making a plea to the world leaders present in London in 1946, he emphasized the connection between feeling and vision: *An inner voice tells us that, animated by a broad and sincere feeling for humanity we can lift up our hearts.*

As the debate grows more profound, I am reminded of one of my mentors in the UN system, the former United Nations Assistant Secretary-General, Zia Rizvi who often echoed the spirit of Angel's call, and spent his career focused on action for refugees around the globe. "No declaration, resolutions or reports would help in the humanitarian field unless and until individuals and nations alike decide to help themselves in making their social environment more humane,"[148] he said.

A sharply intelligent and insightful UN official, Zia Rizvi's book-shelves in his office held titles ranging from international politics to po-etry, philosophy and the great mystics. Just like Prince Aga Khan, with whom he worked for the greater part of his UN service, Rizvi grasped the bigger picture. In 1989, he interviewed me for my first professional position. In the weeks leading up to the interview, I had applied unsuc-cessfully to a number of positions in Geneva after completing my in-ternship. I was only twenty-four years old, so had limited experience to offer. Based on my CV I would fail any competition.

Just as I was contemplating returning to Sweden, giving up my UN dream, and pursuing a law-career back home, I was called for an interview by Zia Rizvi. His deputy wanted a more seasoned candidate who also was a native English-speaker. I was neither, so my odds were slim. But, I had three things to offer. I was a human rights lawyer, I was an amateur poet, and I was equally passionate about both.

"I like you, because you have not only heights, but also depths," Rizvi stated plainly at the end of the interview, extinguishing his Cuban cigar in the ashtray. He recruited me to the Independent Bureau for Humanitarian Issues (IBHI), a UN-affiliated organization established by Prince Aga Khan and Zia Rizvi, from where I moved on into the UN a year later. There began my journey without which this book would not have seen the light of day.

I realize how privileged I was to have worked under Rizvi's lead-ership at the outset of my career. His philosophy resembles the same conclusions drawn by the wise speakers today: "Addressing humanitar-ian problems is a challenge to the mind as well as to the heart. We rec-ognize the limitations of our endeavor. We realize also that feelings and thoughts in themselves are not a substitute for action. But that is where action begins."[149]

Across the gallery, I see many nodding, among them, Helen Keller. She rests the palm of her hand on the left side of her chest, just over her heart. "The keenness of our vision depends not on how much we can see, but on how much we feel."[150] As Keller speaks, there is a sudden sense of collective connection. We are struck by the actual cause and effect: the deeper the feeling, the keener the vision, the more appropriate or responsive will be our action.

"Feelings of passion, pure bliss, reverence, optimism, trust and illumination indicate that your desire to manifest success and abundance has an extremely strong pulling power from the universal source to you,"[151] Dr. Wayne Dyer, says, explaining this higher logic.

Albert Schweitzer nods in agreement. The theologian awarded the Nobel Prize for his philosophy on "reverence for life" stands and takes Dyer's statement further. "By having a reverence for life," Schweitzer says, "We enter into a spiritual relation with the world. By practicing reverence for life we become good, deep, and alive."[152]

We can all relate, for the United Nations' vision is one of reverence for life. It assumes a profound relationship to the world and a universal source. The United Nations proclaims human rights as inherent in human nature and based on natural law. This belief remains a given for most of the participants attending today's session. Kant speaks of the 'moral law within,' Gandhi refers to the 'court of conscience,' and Vaclav Havel calls for a 'change in our consciousness.'

The keenness of their vision is telling.

Gandhi rises from his chair after a long period of silence. He looks around the Chamber to sustain the moment, and then leans forward to speak: "There is something infinitely higher than intellect that rules us and even the sceptics. You must be humble enough to see that in spite of your greatness and gigantic intellect you are but a speck in the universe. A merely intellectual conception of the things of life is not enough. It is the spiritual conception which eludes the intellect, and which alone, can give one satisfaction.[153]" Gandhi takes the dialogue a step further and now speaks of a third form of intelligence: spiritual intelligence.

Unifying our minds, hearts and souls, the mainstream notion of 'spiritual intelligence' was presented by Danah Zohar in 1997 in her book, *ReWiring the Corporate Brain*. The notion involves, among others, the capacity to be vision and value led to act from principles and belief; a holistic understanding, connecting patterns and dots; along with humility and compassion.

Most of the participants today combined their intellect and feelings with spiritual intelligence. Coming from all walks of life, they conceived a value-based vision, were able to connect the dots, and worked with a sense of passion and compassion - ploughing through uncertainties with a great dose of intuition and faith.

"Great men are they who see that the spiritual is stronger than any material force, that thoughts rule the world,"[154] Ralph Waldo Emerson notes. In his most important essay, "Self-Reliance," Emerson argues that there is a genius inside every person. The challenge is to let it out.

Arthur Schopenhauer nods his head, "Every man takes the limits of his own field of vision for the limits of the world." [155] He pauses in an attempt to keep his concerns under wrap, and then resumes, "The more unintelligent a man is, the less mysterious existence seems to him."[156] Schopenhauer rocks the boat a little, but not too much. We can all subscribe to the fact that the United Nations was created out of a vast and value-based vision.

"The United Nations in its fundamental purpose is one of the means by which it is possible for all of us, starting with and in our own lives, to work for that harmony in the world of man which our forefathers were striving for as an echo of the music of the universe."[157] Dag Hammarskjold shares his insights into the grander vision behind the world body. His majestic statement compels us to silence.

The speakers' remarks come from a profound place of immeasurable knowledge. They know that there is a correlation between our sense of purpose, our vision and the way we relate to the starry heavens above us – a correlation that ignites a mighty and supportive force of the universe. Without the capacity to experience this deeper connection, many of today's speakers would not have attained excellence and completion; would not have accomplished what they did for humanity.

"At the moment of commitment the entire universe conspires to assist you," Johann Wolfgang von Goethe, the German writer, poet and statesman, smiles knowingly and echoes the message Hammarskjold has just relayed. Indeed, somewhere, something incredible assisted them to transcend themselves for a noble cause that made a difference to people's lives and for the human family.

We reflect on all these personalities driven by universal values and cooperating with the universe. Many wise poets, scientists, physicians and philosophers have argued for thousands of years that there is a relation between our own attitude and the world around us; a connection between our consciousness and the energy of the universe. Their words remind us that the instant we connect, we access higher knowledge, deeper understanding, and greater energy to manifest those insights.

I look up and realize that the debate has become charged with energy and excitement, prompting Nikola Tesla to take the floor. Immaculately dressed in a three piece suit, the remarkable Serb-American scientist, whose inventions changed the world, speaks from experience. "If you want to find the secrets about the universe, think in terms of energy, frequency and vibration," Tesla explains. "My brain is only a receiver, in the Universe there is a core from which we obtain knowledge, strength and inspiration. I have not penetrated into the secrets of this core, but I know that it exists."[158]

The Chamber has reached a juncture in the debate where metaphysics and quantum physics converge. A world disconnected has yet to make the connection. There comes a time in our service when we will have to step outside ourselves by going deeper within. There comes a point when we have to rise above the confines of conformity and, even reason, to do what needs to be done. There is a fork in the road, and this is the time. Our vision and mission demand a deeper, larger and more expansive human being – not one only able to conceive, but also to receive. For, as Helen Keller says, "The infinite wonders of the universe are revealed to us in exact measure as we are capable of receiving them[159]."

*

Immeasurable knowledge was present at the outset of the United Nations. The founders used their minds, hearts and souls to speak a new language and deliver a new promise to the world. In the aftermath of World War II, with fresh and raw wounds still open, the founders of the United Nations brought purpose to the meaningless. They knew that if life has meaning, the meaning of inhumanity is to work for greater humanity. If things happen for a reason, the reason for injustice is to motivate greater justice. "To conclude this discussion, assessment of justice demands engagement with the 'eyes of mankind,'"[160] Amartya Sen summarizes eloquently.

"But how do we get there?" we ask ourselves as we watch these mysteries unfold through the speakers. It seems that nothing spurs a great vision as much as a great tragedy. This was the destiny of those gathering in San Francisco in 1945.

"We had all these delegates who had just left war-devastated European countries, people who had been living for years without lights, without food. Some of them had come to San Francisco from prison camps," says one staff member who was present in San Francisco. [161]

The Chamber listens. The atmosphere is one of collective remembrance. The whole world had been at war. War-crimes, concentration camps, labor camps, occupation and even the use of nuclear power marked World War II. Entire cities lay in ruins. Somewhere between fifty million and eighty-five million people had perished. The United Nations rose from the ashes of destruction, and created a magnificent vision for all of humankind.

"Out of suffering have emerged the strongest souls; the most massive characters are seared with scars,"[162] Khalil Gibran reflects, loudly, on the forces that inspired the creation of the world body.

"There is no coming to consciousness without pain. In all chaos there is cosmos, in all disorder a secret order" Carl Jung says, explaining the duality so necessary to understanding in today's world too.

Their comments remind us that we may need to go deeper in order to reach higher. We may need to break through our fears to face the consequences of moral and ethical choices in our world today. In an era where the 'will to power' prevails, where violence begets violence, and destruction is applied in response to destruction, something new needs to arise. We are reaching a threshold. Only a great purpose can raze those fears, and change the course of a world so divided. Out of the chaos caused by "the will to power," we can take the leap and choose the 'will to humanity.' This choice depends less on the reason of the head, and more on our capacity to unleash the strength and inspiration residing in our hearts and souls.

Arthur Schopenhauer leans forward and offers an appropriate conclusion. "Nature shows that with the growth of intelligence comes increased capacity for pain, and it is only with the highest degree of intelligence that suffering reaches its supreme point."[163]

The establishment of the United Nations was a supreme moment in our history.

*

The vision of the United Nations broke new ground and reminded us what really matters. It was articulated by human beings who had been to the depths of despair. People who had a glimpse of what was valid and true; who transcended national interest and self-interest during precious moments of enlightened responsibility. Their vision is more real than the world to which we currently subscribe. The founders of the United Nations were imaginative. They chose creation and, in so do-ing, brought completeness to life.

"The more boundless your vision, the more real you are,"[164] says Deepak Chopra, the bestselling author and lecturer, whose writings cast light on our underutilized capacities in the quest for completeness. These are capacities that delivered the vision of the United Nations, as the founders proclaimed the United Nations Charter and the Universal Declaration of Human Rights in the aftermath of World War II.

As we stand on the doorstep to a similar, though successive, de-generation and, perhaps also, eventual collapse, we need to remember and revive that which shaped the vision.

"Respect for the word is the first requirement through which a human being can be nurtured to maturity, intellectually, emotionally, morally,"[165] Hammarskjold leans forward and remarks. His words are reaffirmed by the next speaker.

"What is now wanted is a combination of the greatest heart with the highest intellectuality, of infinite love with infinite knowledge," Vi-vekananda states in closing.

Indeed, in the quest for completeness of life, this is the human being who taps into infinite or immeasurable knowledge to translate words into action, and a vision into reality. But how do we access this knowledge?

"To understand the immeasurable, the mind must be extraordi-narily quiet, still,"[166] Krishnamurti chimes in glancing at Lau Tzu.

"To a mind that is still, the whole universe surrenders," Lao Tzu responds with a smile, as he complements his Indian neighbor.

Yet, another truth has been served to us. We cannot attain our standards of achievement as long as our busy minds look for refuge in the shallow comfort zone. Instead, we ought to be busy seeking comfort and refuge in the stillness of the mind. Many of today's participants knew this, not least Dag Hammarskjold.

During his tenure as the United Nations Secretary-General, Hammarskjold established a meditation room in the United Nations Headquarters in New York. Keenly aware that his position did not bring him the capacities necessary to attain a great vision, Hammarskjold realized it was his responsibility to nurture those capacities in himself, and bring them to his position.

Now, he takes the floor and concludes the discussion. "The more faithfully you listen to the voice within you, the better you will hear what is sounding outside."[167] Calm is the soul that is emptied of all self."[168]

This is the doorway to immeasurable knowledge. While the passionate heart touches the sky, the meditative mind enters it. Through contemplation and meditation we become a reflection of the soul, rather than the head.

And in the soul dwells a greater mind.

# Agenda Item 6
# Hope and Belief: Kindling the Light

*" Don't you know yet? It is your Light that lights the world. "*

*Rumi*

"It always seems impossible until it is done.[169] There is no passion to be found playing small – in settling for a life that is less than the one you are capable of living,"[170] says Nelson Mandela in his unmistakable voice, both confident and humble. We listen to him in awe. This is not the first time Mandela has spoken to the Council. I still remember the feeling of wonder as he entered the Chamber on another occasion a few years ago. I sat in the gallery watching him from afar. We held our breaths. Mandela's living example overcomes all reason.

"I am fundamentally an optimist. Whether that comes from nature or nurture, I cannot say. Part of being optimistic is keeping one's head pointed toward the sun, one's feet moving forward. There were many dark moments when my faith in humanity was sorely tested, but I would not and could not give myself up to despair. That way lays defeat and death," [171] Mandela concludes his illuminating remarks.

Hammarskjold, who like Mandela, defended our universal values and gained respect for doing so, takes the floor, "Never look down to test the ground before taking the next step: only he who keeps his eyes fixed on the far horizon will find the right road,"[172] he reaffirms. During his eight years as the Secretary-General of the United Nations, the youngest ever, Hammarskjold did not let his beliefs be swayed as a result of pressure from any Member State, and was consequently respected by them. Refusing to depart from United Nations' ideals and values, he made ethical politics not only possible, but also favorable and esteemed.

Their words inject a much needed dose of hope in today's debate. We all know that the very survival of the United Nations' vision of international peace and security, and universal human rights and freedoms, depends on this kind of *extraordinary* belief and faith. Optimism is necessary to withstand constant pressure and challenges. Visionary realists are needed: those who are ready to match the requirement of a vision *through the workings of their souls in the way of excellence in a complete life*, to paraphrase Aristotle. It is then that belief and hope are honored as a force of strength rather than a weakness: idealism becomes realistic.

"I think idealism is the only form of realism because unless you're idealistic to some extent, you don't have anything to look forward to, you don't have anywhere to go. And I think there's no point in being pessimistic," [173] says Brian Urquhart, one of the founders of the United Nations, who served the world body for four decades and authored the comprehensive biography, *Hammarskjold*. Dag Hammarskjold remains one of the most astounding examples of a visionary realist who persistently worked through his inner being to align with a vision.

"Surely, in the light of history, it is more intelligent to hope rather than to fear, to try rather than not to try," another visionary realist, Eleanor Roosevelt, complements Urquhart's words. She continues, "For one thing we know beyond all doubt: Nothing has ever been achieved by the person who says, 'It can't be done'." [174]

This is realism in its most progressive form. It is a deep-held sense of personal responsibility that inspires hope and transforms idealism into action. Such was the disposition of the founders of the United Nations.

"Use every letter you write, every conversation you have, every meeting you attend, to express your fundamental beliefs and dreams.

Affirm to others the vision of the world you want. You are a free, immensely powerful source of life and goodness. Affirm it. Spread it. Radiate it. Think day and night about it and you will see a miracle happen: the greatness of your own life,"[175] says Robert Muller, another Assistant-Secretary-General who served with the United Nations for forty years.

Living and manifesting his values of hope and belief, Muller was instrumental in conceiving a number of United Nations agencies, such as the World Food Programme and United Nations Development Programme. He also co-founded and led the United Nations University of Peace in Costa Rica, was a candidate for the United Nations Secretary-General in 1996, and was nominated several times for the Noble Peace Prize.

I first discovered Robert Muller in 1988, at the age of twenty-four. I had just joined the United Nations in Geneva when I came across his book *Most of All, they Taught me Happiness* in which he recollects his service with the United Nations with an encouraging message of turning challenges into opportunity, and despair into hope. I was inspired and went on to read most of his books, motivated by his vision and positive energy. This was the United Nations I had dreamt of serving and the dream had come true.

Time passed. I assumed my first professional post with the United Nations in 1989 and continued my UN career in various crisis countries. A decade later, my friend, Charmaine Crockett, a human rights advocate, and I organized a panel on "The Soul of Human Rights" at the United Nations Headquarters in New York City. Robert Muller accepted our invitation to participate. I found myself seated next to him, jointly delivering this inspiring message before a packed auditorium at the United Nations Headquarters in New York.

Ten years earlier, when first picking up his books, I had no idea that I would meet Muller in person, let alone under such circumstances. Once more I was reminded that when individuals at all levels in an organization or society share the same hope, optimism and dream, the magnetic force of life (and the universe) bring them together, or like Tesla said, *think in terms of energy and frequency.*

In conflict affected countries, I have seen people coming together through a shared sense of hope and belief, turning values into action in the most difficult situations. Thousands of United Nations civil servants work tirelessly in war zones to find solutions. With a great sense of service, United Nations staff from across the system: humanitarians, development personnel, human rights lawyers and peacekeepers, bring hope to millions and make the impossible possible.

"It is about people, this is what motivates me" a colleague from the World Food Programme (WFP) said. Where we relate to people, rather than numbers, unseen possibilities unfold. This is the most distinct difference between the 'will to humanity' and the 'will to power.' When we see clearly what really matters – human beings - and act on this clarity, the *universe conspires to assist us,* to paraphrase Goethe.

Captain Mbaye, a Senegalese United Nations Military Observer, saw clearly and took action, though his story is less well-known. Serving with the United Nations in Rwanda during the genocide in 1994, Captain Mbaye is believed to have saved several hundred possibly over a thousand, lives during the genocide in Rwanda before he was eventually hit by a mortar. "You cannot kill these people, they are my responsibility. I will not allow you to harm them - you'll have to kill me first"[176] Captain Mbaye told the militia, who was blocking his convoy transporting a terrified family to safety.

"He had a sense of humanity that went well beyond orders, well beyond any mandate, [177]" says General Dallaire of his late colleague, reminding us, once more, of the essence.

United Nations staff serving in East Timor during the armed violence in 1999 acted in a similar spirit. Driven by a sense of personal responsibility, they made policies fit people rather than the reverse.

As a result, these UN civil servants saved 1,500 East Timorese when armed militia attacked Dili, following the referendum for independence. Instead of evacuating, as per the stipulated policy, they risked their lives and remained with the terrified displaced population seeking protection in the UN compound. When the UN eventually had to evacuate, they took all the people with them to safety in Australia for temporary protection. This was a hitherto unseen possibility in the work of the UN.

Through sheer determination, unconcerned with glory and even their own lives, theirs is an inspiring example of United Nations international civil servants choosing the 'will to humanity,' placing natural law above positive law where these two conflict, and moral courage above blind obedience. These individuals reaffirmed the founding principles of the United Nations by the choices they made in the face of great danger.

"Reaffirming faith in the basic human impulses which have ensured our survival and progress is, however, essential. Hope is one of those impulses. And humankind needs to nurture and strengthen it in this age more than ever before in its history," [178] says Zia Rizvi, who mentored and inspired that kind of hope in the next generation of UN civil servants.

Today, more than ever, we are aware that it is indeed a matter of survival. In the world of service, of giving and sharing, we can only afford to bring hope and point at hitherto unseen scenarios. We are bound to finally open up space for idealism. Anything less will not do to meet the challenges before us. Moreover, it will be counterproductive, if not also depressingly destructive.

"People who say it cannot be done should not interrupt those who are doing it,"[179] George Bernard Shaw, the highly accomplished and gifted Irish playwright, states confidently, his arms crossed. A co-founder of the London School of Economics, Shaw went on to receive both the Nobel Prize in Literature and an Academy Award. His lifetime's accomplishments and achievements paved the way for new opportunities.

The Chamber observes the speakers as their insights and experiences unfold before us. We watch and listen with a sense of a lingering self-examination. How often do we say or hear that something cannot be done, unless certain conditions are first fulfilled? We have all experienced a sense of frustration when someone claims that the possible "is not possible," then acting on this limited mind set to the detriment of hope. Opportunities lost. Humanity lost.

"Most people spend more time and energy going around problems than in trying to solve them,"[180] Henry Ford stands and looks across the Chamber. "An idealist is a person who helps other people to be prosperous," he remarks. An entrepreneur and well-known optimist, Ford persevered through all manner of difficulties to produce great inventions, while also promoting pacifism for the global family. Contrary to what we often hear, it is possible to do almost anything and be engaged almost everywhere. Everyone can serve and the opportunities are immense.

"One can never consent to creep when one feels an impulse to soar," [181] Keller bursts out. She pauses for a moment and continues in a firm voice, "Optimism is the faith that leads to achievement. Nothing can be done without hope and confidence." [182] With all odds against her, being both deaf and blind, Keller decided to soar. She beat the odds and went on to become a world renowned author, politician and lecturer.

General Dallaire lends support to Keller. "I think that one of the benefits of optimism and idealism is that they lead you into things you would never have tried if you'd let yourself imagine how hard it was going to turn out to be."[183]

As a smile breaks out on her face, Keller concludes, "No pessimist ever discovered the secret of the stars or sailed an unchartered land, or opened a new doorway for the human spirit."

We listen with a deep sense of admiration for all these personalities, who overcame enormous obstacles to take extraordinary action amidst abnormal circumstances. The lesson they transmit to us is that, wherever there are people with hope, working enthusiastically for other people, values translate into action.

"Enthusiasm is one of the most powerful engines of success," Ralph Waldo Emerson exclaims and continues, "When you do a thing, do it with all your might. Put your whole soul into it. Stamp it with your own personality. Be active, be energetic, be enthusiastic and faithful, and you will accomplish your object. Nothing great was ever achieved without enthusiasm." [184] He passes along the same message as Robert Muller, Helen Keller, Dag Hammarskjold, and the many heroes whom I have met in the most difficult circumstances.

One of them is Rev. Dr. Mitri Raheb, the senior pastor of the Evangelical Lutheran Christmas Church in Bethlehem, with whom I have enjoyed many inspiring conversations. "The bridge between immense challenges and a myriad of opportunities is hope in action. Hope is putting what we see into action today. Hope is the power to keep focusing on the larger vision, while taking small, often undramatic steps toward that future."[185]

Dr. Raheb, who is also the president and founder of the Diyar Consortium and Dar al-Kalima University College in Bethlehem, is an internationally acclaimed author and speaker, who serves as the president of Bright Stars of Bethlehem. "Our aim is that our people, who admire stars, will dare to look up and dream, to believe in goals to strive for, and develop a new sense of hope, community, beauty and faith. This is why, for Bright Stars of Bethlehem, hope is what we do!" Dr. Raheb has dedicated his life to providing an environment of creativity and hope for Palestinian youth so that they, amidst the darkness, discover their own light with which to light the world; their own and ours.

"The inner fire is the most important thing mankind possesses,"[186] says a voice from the back of the Chamber. We turn and see the

Finnish poet, Edit Södergran. She wears an elegant dress from the early 1900s with a tall, stiff collar, and a feather in her broad hat. A visionary Swedish-speaking Finnish poet, she speaks of the light within - that which lights the world without.

When probing this light, we realize it is a fire, whose flame does not burn, but brings warmth; and whose rays do not blind, but illuminate. Through hope, this flame transforms adversity into advantage. Through belief, it transcends challenges into opportunity. It burns away the tiers that envelope the sublime - that which is real. Once kindled, it blazes a trail and lights our way.

"Under the sublime law of progress, the present outgrows the past. The great heart of humanity is heaving with the hopes of a brighter day,"[187] someone calls out from the gallery. We turn in his direction. The voice comes from man with ash-blond hair and distinctive facial features. It is Horace Mann, the American politician and educational reformer. Mann championed universal public education and was a staunch opponent of slavery. As a visionary realist, and under the sublime law of progress, his two aspirations were eventually embodied in the Universal Declaration for Human Rights, two centuries later.

*

How much we owe to all these visionaries who are present here today. They put their careers, reputation and comfort at stake to bring hope and belief to others. They were able to grasp that which is sensitive, refined and authentic. Because they perceived the sublime, the unseen possibilities, they kindled a light as the winds of social and political norms tried to extinguish it. This kind of giving, this sort of path, is not an easy one. On the contrary, "To bring the sublime into the mundane is the greatest challenge there is,"[188] Inayat Khan, the poet and founder of the Sufi Order in the West, reminds us.

"All that was great in the past was ridiculed, condemned, combated, suppressed - only to emerge all the more powerfully, all the more triumphantly from the struggle,"[189] says Nikola Tesla offering his wisdom on the subject. His direct and universal experience is echoed by several participants who can relate for they have been there.

As if in chorus, their comments prompt someone else singing the same melody to stand. Vilified, at first, he bounced back and eventually connected the whole world in his own creative way. Steve Jobs emerges from the audience. His voice and message belying his frail physical frame.

"Here is to the crazy ones. The misfits. The rebels. The troublemakers. The round pegs in the square holes. The ones who sees things differently. They are not fond of rules. And they have no respect for the status quo. You can quote them, disagree with them, glorify or vilify them. About the only think you can't do is to ignore them. Because they change things. They push the human race forward. And, while some may see them as the crazy ones, we see genius. Because the people who are crazy enough to think they can change the world, are the ones who do it."[190]

Einstein crosses his arms and smiles. "It gives me great pleasure indeed to see the stubbornness of an incorrigible non-conformist warmly acclaimed."[191]

Enthusiasm spreads infectiously in the Chamber. Some nod silently to one another, while others smile broadly. All can identify - enlightened sages, great political leaders, humanists, scientists and artists. Across different epochs and genres, traversing different continents and cultures, the way their contemporaries viewed them is identical. All were on the edge of losing hope at one point in their lives because the world could not discern the subtle secrets, the great possibilities. They swam against the stream and today the stream turns their direction. They kindled a light and today they light the world in different ways.

"As long as the people don't fear the truth, there is hope,"[192] Alice Walker, the Pulitzer Prize winning author and poet remarks. The author of *The Color Purple* and a courageous political activist brings hope where others dare not tread.

Today, we need these kinds of people more than ever. Individuals who are able to grasp the sublime and, therefore, that which is universally true for the human family. We need to better understand the important role they play for the welfare and progressive evolution of our societies and institutions. We need them in order to reclaim our humanity.

As if reading our minds, Erich Fromm takes the floor and expounds, "The revolutionary and critical thinker is in a certain way always outside of his society while of course he is at the same time also in it. That he is in it is obvious, but why is he outside it? First, because he is not brainwashed by the ruling ideology, that is to say, he has an extraordinary kind of independence of thought and feeling; hence he can have a greater objectivity than the average person has. It seems to me essential that in a certain sense he transcends his society. You may say he transcends it because of the new historical developments and possibilities he is aware of, while the majority still thinks in traditional terms."[193]

As Fromm concludes his insightful analysis, which we would probably have dispensed with in a more commonplace setting, Martin Luther King, Jr. requests the floor. He speaks from experience, "Almost always the creative dedicated minority has made the world better. The question is not whether we will be extremists, but what kind of extremists we will be. The nation and the world are in dire need of creative extremists."[194]

The discussion ceases for a few moments, as we absorb the words of the wise. We have come to a word that needs to be better understood, 'extremism.' A term which does not always mean something bad and despicable. There is more to its definition. Wilberforce declared himself "one of the most incurable *fanatics* ever permitted at large." Beethoven was *possessed* by his art. "Always go *too far*, because that's where you find the truth," Camus said.

We all ought to become more fanatic in our pursuit of humanity.

We need to push farther afield. Because at the other end is the mundane that deprives us of our life force. Millions go to their offices everyday feeling depleted and bored. The flame is slowly being extinguished.

"The worst curse to befall anyone is stagnation, a banal existence, the quiet desperation that comes out of a need for conformity,"[195] Deepak Chopra reminds us calmly, still in his seat.

Indeed, striving for conformity, our fears cannot inspire courage, and our cynicism cannot nurture optimism. To think that it is possible to align these diametrically opposed choices and achieve a vision, or even produce results of any sort, is probably the most accurate definition of "unrealistic expectations."

As the discussion abates leaving room for contemplation, Albert Camus lets out a sigh, "A man devoid of hope and conscious of being so has ceased to belong to the future."[196]

*

We stand at a crossroads. Our institutions and societies need a stimulus of hope and belief to rescue us from the mundane and from silent desperation. Rigid systems with shallow slogans will no longer suffice. Nor will reforming our structures substitute for reforming our attitudes. The heart of the matter runs much deeper than our own image. We are still evolving, still in search of solutions that can match our standards of achievement. For this, we need people who dive deep, dream and dare to do.

"For the future of the world, for its economic growth and human development, there is a need for a new breed of visionary leaders driven by ethics and integrity capable of dreaming the impossible, attracting great ideas, and having the responsibility for believing and committing their lives to them" [197] said Stefano D'Anna, the author of *A Dream for the World*, who is also a world renowned management coach and former leading manager of multinational companies such as Alfa Roméo and Fiat.

Messages of this kind are not abstracts ideals, but the outcome of highly concrete and scientific methods. One of them is the *Appreciative Inquiry* approach (AI), which is gradually making its way into organizations and companies, and has also been introduced to the United Nations. AI developed at Case Western Reserve University by David Cooperrider and Suresh Srivastra, seeking a shift towards a positive-solutions orientation and drawing on all capacities of employees in an organization. *Appreciative Inquiry* empowers through inclusion and inspiration to look for solutions through imagination, feelings, reason and intuition. It is an approach that infuses enthusiasm and thrives on hope.

"We create our organizations based on our anticipations of the future. The image of the future guides the current behavior of any system," Cooperrider said. "It could be argued that all leadership is appreciative leadership. It's the capacity to see the best in the world around us, in our colleagues, and in the groups we are trying to lead. It's the capacity to see the most creative and improbable opportunities in the marketplace. It's the capacity to see with an appreciative eye the true and the good, the better and the possible." [198]

I look around the Chamber. This is the kind of attitudinal change we need in our offices, institutions and societies. In today's extraordinary session on humanity, we are not talking reductionism from a place of pessimism. We are not reducing our noble vision to a flowchart of numbers and figures, at the cost of people and principles. We do not pride ourselves with declaring the glass half full, as opposed to being empty. This attitude will not do justice to the vision we have set for ourselves. "Dream no small dreams for they have no power to move the hearts of men."[199] Goethe articulates the thoughts that so often have crossed my mind over the years.

Today, we are looking at ourselves and our relationship to humanity. We speak from a place where the glass overflows in a vast ocean of possibilities. We are seated firmly in a place of hope and belief, because, says Dr. Raheb, "It is in this time of immense challenges that imaginative faith rises to discover the endless possibilities that lie herein."[200]

Through our vision, we create our reality. The steps unfold via opportunities. The path is paved with choices. But, to seize the opportunities and make the right choices, "You must find the place within yourself where nothing is impossible," Deepak Chopra advises.

Hope and belief are about becoming passionate for all that is positive: to see solutions rather than problems. They are about finding a greater purpose and wholeheartedly pursuing it for the betterment of the human family.

"While this sounds encouraging for the human race, you may be asking yourself: 'What can one person do to truly make a difference in the world?' *Virtually anything!* The only limit to your impact is your imagination and commitment,"[201] Anthony Robbins says energetically and confidently, stretching his arms. Bestselling author of numerous books, including *Awaken the Giant Within*, Robbins' positive philosophy is also applicable and relevant to organizations and systems of service.

It is about pursuing possibilities against the odds, transcending challenges and overcoming obstacles, passionately and persistently. An idea, innovation or solution is only powerful if it is matched by unyielding hope and positive spirit. These are not slogans, but expressions of a character of commitment. Character is not a given, but something we build and shape in our quest for completeness of life.

"Surmounting difficulty is the crucible that forms character,"[202] Robbins notes and passes the floor to Keller, whose own example is more than convincing.

She nods affirmatively and stands saying, "Character cannot be developed in ease and quiet. Only through experience of trial and suffering can the soul be strengthened, vision cleared, ambition inspired, and success achieved."[203]

As Keller seats herself, Theodore Roosevelt picks up on her statement and concludes, "Character, in the long run is the decisive factor in the life of an individual and of nations alike."[204]

Connection made!

The Chamber has moved beyond enthusiasm. We are now in a place of greater awareness and daring wisdom. It is individuals who comprise societies and nations; hence the world. In building our character, it is not by reducing ourselves and our standards that we can bring about a better world, or a *new world,* as Hammarskjold proposed earlier. Rather, it is only by elevating ourselves to the standards we set for the world that we develop a character able to attain that vision.

"Reach high, for stars lie hidden in you. Dream deep, for every dream precedes the goal. Everything comes to us that belongs to us if we create the capacity to receive it,"[205] Rabindranath Tagore, smiles, as we rejoice in the stories of those who have soared before us.

Dots are connected. Threads are woven together. Wisdom is processed. Stillness arrives. As the discussion draws to a close, Rumi stands and gazes across the Chamber. "There is a candle in your heart, ready to be kindled. There is a void in your soul ready to be filled. You feel it, don't you?[206]"

"I am not bound to succeed," Abraham Lincoln adds in conclusion, "but I am bound to live up to whatever light I might have."[207]

The people we serve deserve no less.

# Agenda Item 7
# Freedom and Creativity:
# Telling the Story

" *If you touch one thing with deep awareness, you touch everything.* "

*Thich Nhat Hanh*

Delegates and participants queue by the elevators, while others prefer to take the escalator. Returning from the lunch break, the participants make their way back to the Council Chamber. It's just before 3:00 pm. The wooden doors open wide, and the participants stream into the Chamber.

As the noise of activity settles, the President opens the session's seventh agenda item. His voice is calm and collected. He looks at the big picture - our vision and mission - and urges the Council to examine further factors that might weaken or strengthen our ability to attain the promises we made in 1945.

"With realization of one's own potential and self-confidence in one's ability, one can build a better world,"[208] the Dalai Lama begins. His remarks spur us to penetrate yet another level of understanding. Our collective vision can only be attained through the realization of our own potential.

From the corner of my eye, I see Paul Tillich rise, preparing to make a statement. The German-American theologian is also the author of *The Courage to Be* in which he asserts the need for courage and strength to materialize one's essence and life purpose. In the spirit of his own life and writing, Tillich says, "Man is asked to make of himself what he is supposed to become to fulfill his destiny."[209]

Their statements join together. In attaining our own destiny, we also contribute to fulfilling the destiny of humanity at large – the one envisioned by the United Nations. Conversely, if we do not achieve our individual potential, our collective vision will remain unfulfilled.

Across the aisle, Carl Jung nods in agreement and takes Tillich's statement a step further: "The reason for evil in the world is that people are not able to tell their stories."[210]

The Bohemian-Austrian poet, Rainer Maria Rilke, is next in line and offers the final thought in these introductory remarks. He casts a glance at the previous speakers, and leans forward, "Perhaps every-thing terrible is in its deepest being, something helpless that wants help from us."[211]

Their remarks converge. We see the point. We know that every human being has the potential for making a unique contribution to the world. It is only when we find our purpose in the quest for complete-ness, and thus start toward fulfilling our destiny, that we move from being human to becoming humane, to paraphrase Gandhi. But, when we don't realize our potential the contrary manifests itself. Where po-tential is unfulfilled, there is quiet desperation or even destruction.

Erich Fromm returns to the floor. He removes his glasses and speaks, "The more the drive toward life is thwarted, the stronger is the drive toward destruction; the more life is realized, the less is the strength of destructiveness. Destructiveness is the outcome of an un-lived life."[212]

This is the untold story. And now it shapes a world divided.

As we absorb these opening statements, Nelson Mandela stands, sharing his personal reflections on the matter, "I always knew that deep down in every human heart, there is mercy and generosity. No one is born hating another person because of the color of his skin, or his background, or his religion. People must learn to hate, and if they can learn to hate, they can be taught to love, for love comes more naturally to the human heart than its opposite."[213]

Mandela reaches for his glass of water. For a moment, he is seen quietly contemplating, drawing on his own memories from Robben Island. He resumes and shares a truth with us that alters the way we look at the world, "Even in the grimmest times in prison, when my comrades and I were pushed to our limits, I would see a glimmer of humanity in one of the guards, perhaps just for a second, but it was enough to reassure me and keep me going. Man's goodness is a flame that can be hidden but never extinguished." [214]

The Chamber listens attentively. Mandela speaks of the flame. Edit Södergran's earlier statement rings in the back of our minds: *The inner fire is the most important thing mankind possesses.* They speak of the same flame that ignited the establishment of the United Nations. The UN Charter was crafted around this inner potential "in larger freedom." But it takes freedom from fear to set it ablaze. However, the freedom and creativity that spark this flame often remain quelled - not only collectively, but individually too. It remains an existential human condition still to be conquered.

"Man is born free and everywhere he is in chains,"[215] Rousseau says, as he returns to the discussion. "To renounce freedom is to renounce one's humanity, one's rights as a man and equally one's duties." As the philosophical force behind the French Revolution's quest for human dignity and liberty, Rousseau ignited this inner fire for generations to come. Now he reminds us that without freedom there can be no humanity.

Thus, one is impelled to ponder the question: without freedom to experience the inner fire: warmth of heart, illumination of mind and strength of spirit, how can there be humanity?

Immanuel Kant, whose revolutionary philosophy is also reminiscent of that of the United Nations Charter and Universal Declaration, joins the discussion again and sheds light on how we, ourselves, reduce our freedom to become humane, "It is the freedom to make public use of one's reason at every point. But I hear on all sides, 'Do not argue!' The officer says: 'Do not argue but drill!' The tax collector: 'Do not argue but pay!' The cleric: 'Do not argue but believe!' Only one prince in the world says, 'Argue as much as you will, and about what you will, but obey!' Everywhere there is restriction on freedom,"[216] Kant speaks convincingly, unable to conceal his frustration.

Erich Fromm stands. A profound humanist, like Kant and Rousseau, he explains, "modern man, still is anxious and tempted to surrender his freedom to dictators of all kinds, or to lose it by transforming himself into a small cog in the machine, well fed, and well clothed, yet not a free man but an automaton."[217]

Spurred by Fromm's statement, Aleksandr Solzhenitsyn takes the floor and exclaims with a firm voice: "Only those who decline to scramble up the career ladder are interesting as human beings. Nothing is more boring than a man with a career."[218] As with many of the speakers, he does not mince his words.

Whispering can be heard in the Chamber. I note a few faces showing disapproval, while others ponder quietly. We all look at each other. We are those human beings. I reflect for a moment. Haven't we all thought those thoughts at some point? That external rewards, promotions, position and paycheck, may inadvertently keep us shackled from finding our own story, our unique and optimal gift to humanity? Not because these factors are at fault, per se, but because the unspoken conditions attached to them assume a surrender of our freedom and creativity to accommodate the 'will to power.'

The President of the Council makes the connection. He turns his head towards Abraham Maslow in the front row, suggesting that we review *Maslow's Hierarchy* of needs, which looks at human motivation and growth. Presented in full in 1954 in his book *Motivation and Personality*, Maslow's theory employs positive examples in the form of inspiring personalities, such as Eleanor Roosevelt, Albert Einstein and Frederick Douglass, to explain his theory of self-realization.

Maslow turns on his microphone. We watch in anticipation as a big screen unfolds in the Security Council Chamber and the lights are turned off. We look at the screen with curiosity, and study the pyramid of *Maslow's Hierarchy*, where self-actualization, that would include creativity, is the aspiration at the top of the pyramid, and security, such as may be found in employment, is at the base.

"Every human being has both sets of forces within him" says Abraham Maslow beginning off his brief presentation. Referring to Fromm's and Mandela's remarks, he explains in detail: "One set clings to safety and defensiveness out of fear, tending to regress backward, hanging on to the past, afraid to take chances, afraid to jeopardize what he already has, afraid of independence, freedom and separateness. The other set of forces impels him forward toward wholeness of Self and uniqueness of Self, toward full functioning of all his capacities, toward confidence in the face of the external world at the same time that he can accept his deepest, real, unconscious Self."[219] Maslow takes a deep breath and turns his head towards the participants in the gallery.

"The key question isn't "What fosters creativity?" Maslow lifts his eyebrows, but, "Where was the human potential lost? How was it crippled?"[220]

As Maslow concludes his presentation, leaning back in his chair, we all sense the answer. Wherever we find ourselves in this pyramid is influenced by either the 'will to humanity' or the 'will to power.' The 'will to power' places a large part of the world population at the base. Those who are concerned with sheer physical survival.

"They [the poorest] remain poor because they do not have the opportunities to turn their creativity into sustainable income,"[221] says Mohammad Yunus, the Bangladeshi economist awarded the Nobel Peace Prize for his creative work in eliminating poverty through em-powerment of the poorest.

The 'will to power' also keeps people tied at the base in bureau-cracies and political structures. We are concerned about keeping our jobs and securing the next promotion.

"We prepare our students for jobs and careers, but we don't teach them to think as individuals about what kind of world they would create,"[222] Muhammad Yunus offers a final remark.

The statements crystalize. People can't tell their stories because they lack the supportive environment to exercise freedom and creativity towards self-realization. People either remain at the bottom of Maslow's pyramid or they stop short of moving beyond the middle of the pyramid. It is then that we rescind our freedom to achieve self-realization, hence the attainment of our collective vision, or as Paul Tillich notes, "Man is free even from his freedom; that is, he can surrender his humanity."[223]

"We need freedom to think, to lead and to invest in ourselves for the benefit of others in pursuit of a better world. Out with the old and trodden paths constructed for tactics and gamesmanship, and in with new thinking drawing on the best minds, their convictions and creativi-ty," says Sigrid Kaag, an Under-Secretary-General of the United Nations.

Over the past ten years, Kaag's paths and mine have crossed in various crisis situations. Close up, I have seen Kaag, a mother of four, plow through the most difficult and complex challenges, such as lead-ing the campaign to remove chemical weapons in Syria. In her typical spirit of fearless leadership, she concludes, "In understanding the lives of others, we may need to re-construct a new moral compass which tells the story and charters the journey of a better world- with freedom and creativity it may just be in reach....."

Collectively, it seems that the greatest of all fears is our fear of freedom. This form of fear is the real threat to daringly serve *with* humanity. Often, traditional structures fear freedom, just as the 'will to power' fears humanity. Few people can tell their story in a rigid structure or a confining environment pulling them down into disempowerment and poverty. Where there is no space for creativity, it is difficult to make a unique contribution to the human family.

And yet, there is more to the notion of freedom. For the minds that are truly free create their own space. In the final analysis, freedom is not a place but, rather, a state of mind. Those who possess inner freedom are more likely to choose the 'will to humanity.' When all else has been taken away from them, when they have nowhere else to go, they uncover freedom within and tell their story.

I visited Gaza for the first time in 2010. A year earlier, in 2009, Gaza had been under heavy bombing. In the aftermath of the destruction, people collected debris from destroyed homes, which was processed through a crusher and transformed into fine stones, used to repair and pave new roads. An old man who owned a greenhouse had had all his plants flattened by tanks. In response he went out and gathered new seedlings, the flowers of which were now blossoming in his greenhouse.

The stories were many. People turned destruction into construction; death into life; darkness into light. We ask ourselves: could a human being aspire to a higher and more refined response to the devastation that has been done to them?!

People suffering from violence and injustice possess a resilience and creativity that runs deeper than the average person not confronted with such fate. Inexplicable beauty is created in response to unspeakable cruelty. The 'will to power' may dehumanize a people. But the 'will to humanity' empowers them to become even more humane.

Aleksandr Solzhenitsyn comes forward and speaks from his experience of incarceration in Soviet labor camps, "Bless you prison, bless you for being in my life. For there, lying upon the rotting prison straw, I came to realize that the object of life is not prosperity as we are made to believe, but the maturity of the human soul."[224] His earlier statement now makes sense. In the comfort zone nothing grows, lest from within.

"To be a light to others you will need a good dose of the spiritual life. Because as my mother used to say, if you are in a good place, then you can help others; but if you're not well, then go look for somebody who is in a good place who can help you,"[225] Rigoberta Menchu advises. A Nobel Prize Laureate and empowering leader for the indigenous people of Guatemala, I met this remarkable woman in 2010. Her life was lived outside the comfort zone, while mine was inside, but our discussion over lunch in Guatemala City was one of inspiration and humility. Unless we ignite the fire within, how can we light the world without?

Following upon Menchu's statement, Erich Fromm returns to the discussion and shares the universal truth spoken by earlier speakers. Like theirs, his words bear strong resemblance to the founding spirit of the United Nations.

"Man's main task in life is to give birth to himself, to become what he potentially is. The most important product of his efforts is his own personality. The quest for certainty blocks the search for meaning. Uncertainty is the very condition to impel a man to unfold his power. I believe that if an individual is not on the path to transcending his society and seeing in what way it furthers or impedes the development of human potential, he cannot enter into intimate contact with his humanity." [226]

Fromm pauses and then concludes, "I believe that society, while having a function both stimulating and inhibiting at the same time, has always been in conflict with humanity. Only when the purpose of society is identified with that of humanity will society cease to paralyze man and encourage his dominance."[227]

We reflect, silently. In a world dominated by the 'will to power,' we step on others at the lower base of the pyramid to reach the top. It is an illusion though, for there can be no self-realization where there is no 'other-realization.' We cannot tell our story by silencing others. It is only in helping others climb up from the base that we can realize ourselves and truly serve society and the world.

"No man can put a chain about the ankle of his fellow man without at last finding the other end fastened about his own neck,"[228] Frederick Douglass takes the floor. By telling his story, Douglass helped millions identify with their humanity. Born into slavery in 1818 on a plantation in Maryland, Douglass' refusal to accept slavery inspired his flight to freedom. He then went on to become the leader of the abolitionist movement that inspired an end to slavery.

"To be free is not merely to cast off one's own chains, but to live in a way that respects and enhances the freedom of others,"[229] says Nelson Mandela, who, in the same spirit as Douglass, told his story of liberating others. "I am not truly free if I am taking away someone else's freedom, just as surely as I am not free when my freedom is taken from me. The oppressed and the oppressor alike are robbed of their humanity."

Quietly and contemplatively, Dag Hammarskjold distils the gist of the discussion, "No peace which is not peace for all. No rest until all has been fulfilled."[230]

*

A mature soul is a soul that is in intimate contact with his or her humanity. The mature soul cannot compromise on freedom and creativity because freedom and creativity are about giving with our souls, minds and hearts in a moment of absolute connection and completness.

The story of the mature soul is one that touches all with profound awareness and enables others to attain their humanity too. The mature soul sustains the glimpse. The United Nations was established to achieve this maturity. Through the United Nations Charter and the Universal Declaration for Human Rights, a collective effort was made to support each individual to attain their potential for becoming fully humane in 'larger freedom.'

"Everybody has a creative potential and from the moment you can express this creative potential, you can start changing the world,"[231] I overhear Paolo Coelho whispering to Horace Mann, who sits on his right. Mann leans left and nods, "The living soul of a person once conscious of its power cannot be quelled."[232]

This is the power of humanity. It is in attaining this maturity that we become fit for purpose. When we touch that purpose and freedom deep within ourselves, we touch all humanity.

It begins there and it begins with every person who constitutes, "We, the people" of the United Nations, every individual for whom the Universal Declaration for human rights was created. That means some seven billion people dwelling on this planet. The responsibility rests on all of us currently claiming space - or confining the space of others - to tell the story.

"Our duty is to encourage everyone in his struggle to live up to his own highest idea, and strive at the same time to make the ideal as near as possible to the Truth,"[233] Vivekananda stands and says in a gentle voice. He probes further and continues, "You have to grow from inside out. Dare to be free, dare to go as far as your thought leads, and dare to carry that out in life. Don't look back—forward, infinite energy, infinite enthusiasm, infinite daring, and infinite patience—then alone can great deeds be accomplished."

As the discussion draws to a close, Rumi rises and speaks softly, "Everyone has been made for some particular work, and the desire for that work has been put in every heart," he says, raising his voice, "Seek the wisdom that will untie your knot. Seek the path that demands your whole being."[234]

Anaïs Nin smiles, "Then the day came, when the risk to remain tight in a bud was more painful than the risk it took to blossom." [235]

Poets can indeed change the world.

# *Agenda Item 8*
# *Individuals and Growth:*
# *Remaking Ourselves*

" *If you are what you should be, you will set the whole world on fire.* "

*Catherine of Siena*

"The difference between what we do and what we are capable of doing would suffice to solve most of the world's problems,"[236] says Gandhi beginning the next agenda item with this enticing statement. While he speaks in a measured tone, his message sees no boundaries, other than the limitations we impose on ourselves.

"As human beings," he continues, "our greatness lies not so much in being able to remake the world - that is the myth of the atomic age - as in being able to remake ourselves."[237] Gandhi's slight frame gives no hint of the giant within. He lived his message.

Across the aisle, George Bernard Shaw stretches his open palms towards Gandhi and nods, "There can be no progress in the world without personal progress. No evolution without inner growth."[238]

It dawns on us that they think alike. Politics, art, science and mysticism intertwined. East and West meet. Their lessons and messages are universal. It is in remaking ourselves that we change the world: the potential realized and the story told. From there, the state of the world manifests itself and the aspirations of the United Nations materialize. These are the laws that govern human nature and those of the universe. Somewhere, it all connects through a higher logic.

"Our work for peace must begin with the private world of each one of us. To build for man a world without fear, we must be without fear. To build a world of justice, we must be just. And how can we fight for liberty if we are not free in our own minds? How can we ask others to sacrifice if we are not ready to do so?"[239] Hammarskjold shares his insights into this logic, as others come forward to reaffirm his statement.

A woman stands and slowly walks towards the horseshoe table while leaning on her cane. She stops. Her eyes greet each and every one of the diplomats around the table with a silent nod. She turns towards the participants in the auditorium. Mother Theresa speaks, "It starts with ourselves, and spreads like rings on the water."[240] As she takes her seat, Eleanor Roosevelt rises behind her.

Roosevelt holds the Universal Declaration in her right hand. "Where, after all, do universal human rights begin? In small places, close to home - so close and so small that they cannot be seen on any maps of the world. Yet they are the world of the individual person; the neighborhood he lives in; the school or college he attends; the factory, farm, or office where he works. Such are the places where every man, woman, and child seeks equal justice, equal opportunity, equal dignity without discrimination. Unless these rights have meaning there, they have little meaning anywhere. Without concerted citizen action to uphold them close to home, we shall look in vain for progress in the larger world."[241]

Their message is clear: we are defined by the way we relate to other people, which also reflects our own growth, the way we respond to our experiences, the way we learn from our mistakes; and, the determination that drives us to change and evolve. It is when we decide to bring that vast vision and mission into ourselves and our daily lives that we will truly reform and progress.

"As I near the end of my employment with the United Nations as a humanitarian actor, I am able to draw upon a deep wealth of experiences - moments of tumultuous joy when refugees are finally able to return to their homes and regain their dignity.....as well as many painful memories of tragedies, witnessing genocide and massacres," says Neill Wright, the former UN Humanitarian Coordinator in war ravaged Iraq. Serving as Wright's deputy at the UN's High Commission for Refugees (UNHCR) in the Balkans in the 1990s, I saw a person consistently taking decisions that would improve people's lives. "Is humankind able to change and to learn from its mistakes?" he asks as he completes his last term of UN duty. "We all need to take some time each day to watch the sunrise and restore faith that we can make a difference."

Indeed, we need to restore our faith again and again through a broader and more expansive understanding that connects us to the world. While we seek to comprehend our budgets and organizational structures, we also need to understand human existence. While we are familiar with the statistics of wars, we also need to know the pain of the millions enduring those wars. Because it is only when we seek to understand our tendancy for inhumanity as much as our potential for humanity that we will truly begin to learn from our mistakes.

"To know humanity, understand earth; to know earth, understand heaven; to know heaven, understand the way; to know the way, understand the great within yourself,"[242] says Lao Tzu delivering an essential piece of advice. His statement sparks further reflection in the Chamber.

This time, we do not look at each other to measure reactions. We look at ourselves from inside out. One of the most universal truths has just been described by the speakers: the Greek aphorism, "Know Thyself." This is the essence of growth and evolution. It is the force and process, inasmuch as the goal of change. "Know Thyself" - these two words are key to creating *one world*. How did we miss the point?

"Most persons are so absorbed in the contemplation of the outside world that they are wholly oblivious to what is passing on within themselves,"[243] Nikola Tesla speaks calmly. His voice carries no judgment. It is a reality to which most can relate.

We prefer external comfort before internal change. We tend to adjust to 'the 'will to power" and defer 'the 'will to humanity.' Change and growth become a chronic debt to ourselves. But, since the world does not change unless we change, it is eventually life that changes us.

Silence permeates the Chamber. Once more, we identify - the diplomat, the civil servant, the politician and the rest of humanity. We know that change is inevitable to cope with the mounting challenges of a world mired in deep divisions. And, we know that it hinges on us as individuals too.

"To move the world we must move ourselves. In all of us, even in good men, there is a lawless wild-beast nature, which peers out in sleep,"[244] says Socrates illuminating the debate.

We soak up his words. We see that the path to the unknown field leads us back to ourselves. Within us lies the pasture of potential and purpose. Within us also lies the battlefield between the small self and the larger self. The inward journey of growth and evolution for the human family is through that field.

"We never know how high we are till we are called to rise. Then if we are true to form our statures touch the skies,"[245] Emily Dickinson, the gifted American poet, declares and stretches out her right arm, pointing at the ceiling.

Their words speak both of a challenge and an opportunity. It takes courage to leave the comfort zone and tread into the unknown field. It takes courage to surrender the ego and make the connection to humanity, our own and that of the rest of the world.

"Would you like to save the world from the degradation and destruction it seems destined for?" Lao Tzu asks. "Then step away from shallow mass movements and quietly go to work on your own self-awareness. If you want to awaken all of humanity, then awaken all of yourself."[246]

This awakening is a process of transformation, as Meister Eckhart explains, "A human being has so many skins inside, covering the depths of the heart. We know so many things, but we don't know ourselves! Why, thirty or forty skins or hides, as thick and hard as an ox's or bear's, cover the soul. Go into your own ground and learn to know yourself there."[247]

Once we choose the 'will to humanity,' we can learn from people suffering conflict and injustice – be they the founders of the United Nations or the billions enduring injustice, violence and poverty around the globe. For it is they who are most inclined to walk this path. Victims of the 'will to power' are often spurred to find a greater power in their own humanity, as their life constantly forces them to go inward.

"The best way to find yourself is to lose yourself in the service of others,"[248] Gandhi whispers to Alice Walker, sitting to his left.

Walker grabs his wrist gently and reassuringly. "I think that all people who feel that there is injustice in the world anywhere should learn as much of it as they can bear. That is our duty."[249]

Dr. Ali Khashan is the former Minister of Justice of the Palestinian Authority. A refugee, born in Jerusalem, his family had fled the violence of 1948. "I have never known my hometown," he says in a calm and factual tone. He grew up in the camps. "Amidst the darkness around me, a light was set aflame within me. It was a light of hope and it inspired me to search."

As a child, he wrote poetry. In high school he heard about the notions of freedom and constitutional rights which led him to find books on Rousseau and Montesquieu. From writing poetry, he moved on and devoted his time to reading and reflection. "Slowly it transpired before me," says Dr. Khashan, "that freedom was not only a noble ideal. It was a right".

In his search, Dr. Khashan also read Arabic philosophy, including the comprehensive *Al-Muqaddimah*, by Ibn Khaldun. He began to see that freedom was not solely a French or Western concept. It was universal and belonged to all people. He knew in his heart that he would rise out of his confining existence and become something. Yet little did he realize that one day he would become the Minister of Justice to the Palestinian Authority, a professor of Constitutional Law and the founder of Al Quds Law School.

A close friend, since his days in the Palestinian Ministry of Justice when we jointly established a major United Nations rule of law assistance programme for the Palestinian people, Dr. Khashan has taught me a great deal about patience and faith, "Knock on the door of justice and freedom again and again," he says, "Do not give up. Because when freedom and justice come from within, the door will eventually open."

Perhaps the day we choose to learn from those on the other side of the fence, when we honor humanity more than power, we will realize that the comfort zone is a resting place, not a place of dynamic growth. That everything going our way is a curse, not a blessing, and that facing suffering, that of others or our own, brings wisdom, grace and gratitude.

The young man sits in a wheelchair in the yard of the International Red Cross hospital in Kabul, swatting the flies away from his injuries. I spot him from afar and approach him. Shattered by the sight of his open wounds, I collect myself and begin a conversation with him. He tells me his story. He was playing with some friends under a tree, when he stepped on a mine and lost the use of his limbs. Yet he smiles.

"What makes you smile that beautiful smile?" I ask. He does not answer at first but keeps swatting the flies, a smile on his face. I ask again.

Siddiqula looks at me with his big almond-shaped eyes. "When I stepped on that mine, God saved my life."

That evening, I cried. I asked myself what sense it makes to hold righteousness in our hands on the safe side of the fence, while others lose their limbs on the frontline while holding on to all that they have left, righteousness in their hearts?

*

"There is only one perpetrator of evil on the planet: human unconsciousness," Eckhart Tolle says from the gallery [250]. His statement echoes Vaclav Havel's plea at the outset of today's session: *Without a global revolution in the sphere of human consciousness, nothing will change for the better...*

Today, we see a growing awareness of our consciousness. More and more people embark on the inner journey through mindfulness and a greater quest for clarity and wisdom, within. Many now realize that there is something far above our own small egos and selves, our nations or regions. This growing awareness of our interconnection as individuals, societies and nations is increasingly linked to leadership, civil society, economic affairs, politics and governance.

Such awareness in a large organization, like the United Nations, is reflected in *A New Humanism for the 21st Century* by Irina Bokova, who heads the United Nations Educational and Scientific and Cultural Organization (UNESCO). She speaks of our individual and collective interconnection towards the world we want, "An accomplished human being is one who recognizes coexistence and equality with all others, however far away, and who strives to find a way to live with them. This new humanism calls for every human being to be able to truly participate in our shared destiny, including the most marginalized among us."[251]

The humanist philosophy is a call for both an individual and collective commitment to the idea of universal human rights, justice and peace – the founding principles of the United Nations. The first premise is the realization that life is not about what we can take from the world, but what we give to the world. This is the fundamental difference between the 'will to power' and the 'will to humanity.' The second premise is to find the particular purpose that will be our gift to humanity. Both, first and foremost, are found within ourselves.

"If your goal is not determined by your most secret pathos, even victory will only make you painfully aware of your own weakness,"[252] Hammarskjold says calmly and confidently, before he continues, "The more faithfully you listen to the voice within you, the better you will hear what is sounding outside."[253] Once more, he gives us the guidance we so urgently need, and so illustrative of his own life and legacy.

In similar vein, Jung chimes in and reaffirms Hammarskjold's statement, "Your vision will become clear only when you can look into your own heart. Who looks outside dreams, who looks inside awakes."[254]

Hammarskjold nods, "To become free and responsible,"[255] he says, before falling silent for a moment. His eyes fixed straight ahead, he concludes, "The longest journey is the journey inwards."[256]

# Agenda Item 9
# Humanity and Service:
# A Spiritual Renaissance

*" The spiritual life does not remove us from the world but leads us deeper into it. "*

Henri J.M. Nouwen

The extraordinary session is coming to an end. It is late afternoon. The Security Council Chamber reflects a spirit of rising hopefulness. The greatest minds and hearts to walk the earth have spoken to the fate of the human family. It is a special occasion. We know that this opportunity will not present itself again.

Those gathered here today stand for justice and freedom, inspiring us to greater deeds. They are the inventive and creative minds, pushing the frontiers of human achievement. They bring vision and hope, kindling a light. They are the conveyers of beauty and splendor, gracing our life on earth. That which they all have in common is their 'will to humanity.' Can we afford to discount their wisdom in the twenty-first century? There is a fork in the road. We have promises to keep, and choices to make.

"Once more we are in a period of uncertainty, of danger, in which not only our own safety but that of all mankind is threatened," Eleanor Roosevelt's warning rings across in the Chamber. As she delivers her final remarks, she makes a timeless appeal: "Once more we need the qualities that inspired the development of the democratic way of life. We need imagination and integrity, courage and a high heart. We need to fan the spark of conviction, which may again inspire the world as we did with our new idea of the dignity and worth of free men. But first we must learn to cast out fear. People who 'view with alarm' never build anything."[257]

Her sage words are neither new, nor old. They are eternal and thus ever so relevant. We are called to define ourselves and our relationship to the world. The choices we make and the paths we take determine who we are and the trail we leave behind for our children. Will we choose the 'will to humanity' or the 'will to power,' or perhaps a configuration of both: the power of humanity? Will we transition from being human to becoming humane?

"The dividing line goes within ourselves, within our own peoples and also within other nations. It does not coincide with any political or geographical boundaries," Dag Hammarskjold rises from his chair and speaks with unmistakable conviction to the Council, "The ultimate fight is the one between the human and the sub-human. We are on dangerous ground if we believe that any individual, any nation, any ideology has monopoly on rightness, liberty and human dignity."[258] Hammarskjold silently returns to his seat. Deep reflection is always present in his life.

The next speaker, Nelson Mandela, steps forward and offers his final remarks. He glances at Hammarskjold as he illustrates the dangerous ground, the weak foundation, upon which the world rests today, "To deny people their human rights is to challenge their very humanity,"[259] Mandela states resolutely. His words echo across the Council entrusted to maintain peace and security in the world.

Images of the world as it is today play out on the screens of our minds. Millions are denied their human rights in armed conflicts that have decimated whole nations, destabilized regions, and divided the world. Whether we are aware or not, whether we connect the dots or remain disconnected, truth stands by itself. We are on dangerous ground because of political selectivity and national interests unaligned with the world's interest, because of fear, greed and selfishness.

The 'will to power' has overtaken our humanity.

Albert Einstein nods affirmatively at Hammarskjold and Mandela, as he requests the floor. He leans forward and wraps up his concluding remarks, "Heroism on command, senseless violence, and all the loathsome nonsense that goes by the name of patriotism – how passionately I hate them."[260] In closing, Einstein shakes his head in exasperation, "Nationalism is an infantile disease. It is the measles of mankind."[261]

His final remarks delivered, the multi-faceted scientist seats himself to give room to the remarkable poet, Rabindranath Tagore, who rises slowly. His voice tranquil, Tagore's words instantly illuminate the Chamber: "Patriotism cannot be our final spiritual shelter; my refuge is humanity. I will not buy glass for the price of diamonds, and I will never allow patriotism to triumph over humanity as long as I live."[262]

Their statements align with our vision and mission. What if their remarks would be uttered by many more; how different the world might be! Their well-chosen words and dispositions belong to those who shall not fail.

I look around. We absorb their insights and appeals. We all ponder the same questions. A profound responsibility rests with the United Nations, the world leaders of all Member States and we, the people. In 2015, the United Nations commemorates its seventieth anniversary. In 2016, the world body will select the next leader to guide us through the unknown field of the twenty-first century. As we choose our leaders, shape our organizations and articulate our policies, billions of human beings will, once more, call on us to value our vision and validate our values. Will we hear their cries and heed their call?

"We have heard the rationales offered by the nuclear superpowers. We know who speaks for the nations. But who speaks for the human species? Who speaks for Earth?"[263] Carl Sagan breaks in, standing up at the center of the gallery. The world renowned scientist and astronomer has quietly followed today's session and now elects to speak, "We are a way for the cosmos to know itself, we make our world significant by the courage of our questions and the depth of our answers."[264] He rests for a moment to allow us to ponder. We wait in anticipation. We yearn to know that "something incredible" waiting to be known.

Sensing our thirst for an answer, Sagan resumes, "Once we overcome our fear of being tiny, we find ourselves on the threshold of a vast and awesome Universe that utterly dwarfs – in time, in space, and in potential,"[265] he says reflectively and then concludes, "The choice is with us still, but the civilization now in jeopardy is all humanity."[266]

Sagan speaks of the mother of all opportunities.

That 'something' is an opportunity so grand and glorious we cannot fully comprehend its force. It encompasses all that is out there, far and beyond, and yet is so near too. We can seize it, for it is within our reach. Sensitive, refined and authentic, it is waiting to be found. It lies within.

The choice still remains with us.

"Every person must decide, at some point, whether they will walk in the light of creative altruism or in the darkness of destructive selfishness. This is the judgment. Life's most persistent and urgent question is, 'What are you doing for others?' " Martin Luther King, Jr. rises and speaks calmly to this choice. He reaffirms that it is within our own purview. It depends on our vision. "An individual has not begun to live until he can rise above the narrow horizons of his particular individualistic concerns to the broader concerns of all humanity." [267]

The Security Council listens. The answer is to be found solely inside ourselves. There where we transcend "them" and "we" through the point of convergence. There, where we realize that national interests cannot overtake the interest of the human family, but ought to align with it. There, where the 'will to power' no longer confines the 'will to humanity,' but converges with it. It is there that we elevate ourselves to a new level of existence. The words from the opening of the first General Assembly in 1946 come to mind once more. They remain as valid today as they did seventy-years ago, 700 years ago or 7,000 years ago. *"An inner voice tells us that, animated by a broad and sincere feeling for humanity, we can lift up our hearts..."*

As we listen to the speakers making their final remarks, I see Dr. Zuleta Angel emerge from the far corner of the auditorium. He has been silent today. He looks across the sea of participants in the crowded Chamber. The President of the Council invites him to speak. Angel greets us with a nod, "The whole word now awaits our decisions, and rightly - yet with understandable anxiety - looks to us now to show ourselves capable of mastering our problems."[268] As Angel sits, we take a moment to deliberate quietly.

The silence breaks again. Vaclav Havel taps lightly on his microphone. Speaking from a place deep within, we can all relate, when he says, "The salvation of this human world lies nowhere else than in the human heart, in the human power to reflect, in human meekness and human responsibility."[269] Touched, we now see clearly.

The participants in today's session number over a hundred and have traveled from afar through time and space to help us find solutions. Throughout the day, their wisdom has gradually aligned, piece by piece, step by step, towards the big picture. It is logical, magnificent and humane all at the same time. Yet, it is simple, and therefore also real.

"What we now want is closer contact and better understanding between individuals and communities all over the earth, and the elimination of egoism and pride which is always prone to plunge the world into primeval barbarism and strife...,"[270] Tesla makes a final appeal. "Peace can only come as a natural consequence of universal enlightenment."[271]

As the speakers deliver their concluding statements, our clichés crumble; our conventional means collapse. Neither can lay the foundation for building a *new world*. They all point in the same direction. The 'will to humanity' rests on a foundation far stronger than the 'will to power.' It is in alignment with the moral law within, that which makes us humane, and it is also aligned with the starry heavens above us, a universe both vast and awesome.

"One truth stands firm, all that happens in world history rests on something spiritual. If the spiritual is strong, it creates world history. If it is weak, it suffers world history,"[272] Albert Schweitzer notes before turning the floor to Inayat Khan.

Khan's eyes are fixed on the distance, as if penetrating the walls. He gazes ahead and above, just as poets do. "The solution to the problem of the day is the awakening of the consciousness of humanity to the divinity within,"[273] he states gently. We remain pensive. What else is left to say?

Their calls have never been as urgent. The wisdom of all gathered here has never been so pressing. Our systems, structures and processes hold us back. Our attitudes and mindsets limit us. Our political agendas do not attain our vision. Something new must arise - something greater and more real than what we have created.

Hammarskjold is invited to offer the final remark of the day's session. He takes a deep breath, and shares with us a concluding plea, one that we can no longer afford to disregard: "Unless there is a spiritual renaissance, the world will know no peace."[274]

The ensuing silence speaks to all of us. In stillness, we are prompted to look within and ahead. My eyes wander across the walls of our offices, to the frontlines of the many wars haunting us today, and into the battlefield of my own inner search. Far above our ceilings, within reach of the sky, I hear a whisper from deep within myself. It yearns to be heard. I close my eyes and listen:

*"*
*In all that you dream to possess and achieve,*
*seek to remove the "I" and the "me."*
*In all that you yearn to become and to be,*
*seek to merge the "they" and the "we."*
*Beyond all that you crave, and all that you wish,*
*there is a greater "What shall be........*
*"The goal of all human life and Thee:*
*Humanity set free.* **"** [275]

The President of the Security Council reads out draft resolution 1964/2015 titled "An Agenda for Humanity." He walks us through the paragraphs of the resolution, representing the agenda items we have discussed, each serving as a building block for a *new world*.

The President calls the fifteen Members of the Council to vote. "Let yourself become living poetry,"[276] Rumi, the traveler, says lightly as the voting begins.

The votes are counted in silence. Resolution 1964 (2015) is adopted unanimously. The President strikes his gavel. Today's session is over. Tomorrow is a new beginning.

The participants rise from their chairs, still thoughtful. They shake hands and exchange smiles. It has been a long day. Outside, the clouds have dispersed and the sun is setting over New York City. People move slowly towards the exit, some resume quiet exchanges, others remain reflective. As the room empties, I spot an elderly man in his seat. He turns around and I glimpse his face. It is the French author, poet and politician, Victor Hugo. He gazes into the distance. The glint in his eyes speaks of our newfound humanity, as he whispers, "All the forces in the world are not so powerful as an idea whose time has come."[277]

# Afterword: Taking the Step
"
*Everything that rises must converge.*
"

*Alice Walker*


This is my story. For twenty-five years it lay within me waiting to be told. I lived through its unwritten pages. Driven by a passion in my work as I stood face to face with inhumanity, on the one hand, and human resilience, on the other, I often retreated into silence and read the words imprinted on my soul – the book waiting to be born.

We never know when life calls us to take a step. When it does, it expects us to be ready. When the time had come for me to write this monograph and I chose to proceed, it took twelve months to materialize.

As I wrote, it became my sanctuary. Most evenings and weekends, I entered the Chamber to listen to the great personalities of our past and present, and allowed myself to reflect, integrate and be inspired. It reminded me, once more, that service is the greatest of human aspirations. There is so much sorrow and injustice in this world that we cannot afford to waste our lives turning a blind eye to humankind's misery. It also reassured me of our human potential and enormous possibilities. It reminded me of what our world could look like. I am convinced that each of us can make a difference in optimal and unique ways.

I believe it is possible. I believe so because of the trustworthiness of these world-renowned personalities participating in this imaginary debate. I believe so because of the people I have met in the harshest circumstances, whose examples of forbearance testify to the fortitude of the human spirit. And, I believe so because I feel it within. I always have.

At the same time, one has to be careful in calling others to rise to a new level of humanity. These are big assumptions. At the end of the day, there can be no expectations but self expectations. We all struggle with our own imperfections. And, we all yearn to tell our story. For this reason, I have tried to maintain consistency throughout the book by referring to us in the first person plural. "We are all in the gutter," as Ralph Waldo Emerson said, "But some of us look up at the stars."

As long as I can remember, dating to my early childhood, and inspired by my parents' profound depth and wisdom, I have looked up at the stars. The stars inspired my choice of profession, my passionate search for answers and, eventually, this book. Irrespective of the circumstances, my sage and beautiful mother always spoke of unseen potentials for growth and unexplored possibilities for service. "I can't explain it, I just *feel* it," she used to say pointing at the stars.

The message of this volume is to remember why we are here. And to ask the questions that will bring us closer to the answer. When we refuse to accept the 'will to power' taking control over people, societies, nations, the world and most of all, ourselves, the answer will find its way to us. Through integration and inspiration, it slowly unfolds before our eyes. We see the big picture. We realize how each piece relates to the other, the interdependence of all there is and how it begins within ourselves.

We make the connection.

It was in this spirit that I wrote these pages which I hope will encourage optimal choices that serve the human family, and, with those, also our own potential. Perhaps the most essential of these choices is to know ourselves and to dig so far down into the soil of our own hearts and souls that we finally unearth the hidden treasure of our humanity. I believe at that point we begin to rise and converge with the humanity of others.

It is then that we will be able to influence and inspire other human beings, organizations and political structures to revive, or shift towards, a humanism so urgently needed in the twenty-first century. It is then that we shall be fit for purpose in meeting contemporary challenges and delivering on our promises, as once articulated by the founders of the United Nations.

This transformation starts the moment we choose the 'will to humanity.'

When talking about humanity we must also have the courage to talk about the human suffering that results from inhumanity caused by the 'will to power.' While violations of international law are classified in legal terms, some more egregious than others, one must never compare suffering. Each person and every people has its own experience, which others can never fully comprehend.

Just as one cannot compare suffering, however, even less can one justify inflicting suffering on others, as a consequence of having suffered oneself. The spell has to be broken. In breaking the spell, we must do so without any interest other than the interest of all humanity. While we may argue the law and disagree on its interpretation, the person of civility will not dispute the essence of international law: justice and humanity.

The suffering on our globe has reached unspeakable proportions and we are going backwards. The divide between cultures, religions and people continues to widen by the day. We have taken the wrong road repeatedly and, eventually, not surprisingly, ended up where we are today. The problem is not different faiths or religions, or diverse cultures or ethnicities. As Leo Tolstoy said: "Faiths, there are many, but of the spirit there is one; in me, in you, and in every man. The sole meaning of life is to serve humanity."

This book makes the case for humanity anywhere and anytime, without distinction or partisanship. The case for humanity is one, in me, in you, in every man and woman, to paraphrase Tolstoy.

Still, since I wrote this volume in Jerusalem, and since the Holy Land finally compelled me to sit down, collect my thoughts, connect the dots and examine my answers, it behooves me to say something about this particular context.

I have lived among Palestinians and Israelis. Both sides experience fear and grievances. I am fully mindful of the fact that I cannot judge the degree of suffering that I have not experienced personally. But, I hold one truth to be certain. I can say with strict impartiality and legal objectivity that the Palestinians are a violated and downtrodden people in this very asymmetric conflict. They are in a struggle, against time, for freedom. Meanwhile, we, on the other side of the fence, are on the verge of losing our humanity. Not until the day we recognize the humanity of the Palestinians – their inherent human rights translated into action - will these two Semitic peoples with so much in common live in peace and mutual respect.

Should we make the choice to heed the wisdom shared by great personalities of different nationalities, ethnicities, and faiths and apply their insights - item by item - consistently and without discrimination, I believe we will also find peace and justice between Palestinians and Israelis. As an old Palestinian man in Hebron, his eyes moist with tears said, "We are all one humanity: we come from the same place and we will go to the same place."

Palestinians need to be set free for the sake of all of us. It is not beyond our reach, since rescuing our humanity is not impossible. The mere notion that it might be otherwise should make us all shiver. It is a choice we make. In the final analysis, it is the degree to which we choose to descend as individuals that will determine the heights to which we will rise and converge with the rest of humanity.

I have hope and as I sometimes say, to my gracious and compassionate colleagues and friends, in Gaza, Ramallah or Bethlehem, who have taught me so much about humanity, one day you will touch the sun with your fingertips and turn the light towards those still in darkness.

May the rest of us – still in darkness on the other side of the wall – be showered by that light and attain the same depth of humanity.

# List of Participants

| | | | | |
|---|---|---|---|---|
| 1 | Sami Abdelshafi | | 29 | Khalil Gibran |
| 2 | John Quincy Adams | | 30 | Johann Wolfgang Goethe |
| 3 | Prince Sadruddin Aga | | 31 | Hafiz |
| 4 | Fehmi Agani | | 32 | Dag Hammarskjold |
| 5 | Aristotle | | 33 | Thich Nhat Hanh |
| 6 | Omar Bakhet | | 34 | Vaclav Havel |
| 8 | Simone de Beauvoir | | 35 | Stephane Hessel |
| 9 | Ludwig van Beethoven | | 36 | José Ramos-Horta |
| 10 | Irina Bokova | | 37 | Victor Hugo |
| 11 | Edmund Burke | | 38 | Steve Jobs |
| 12 | Albert Camus | | 39 | Carl Jung |
| 13 | Deepak Chopra | | 40 | Sigrid Kaag |
| 14 | Paolo Coelho | | 41 | Franz Joséph Kafka |
| 15 | Confucius | | 42 | Immanuel Kant |
| 16 | Jean D'Arc | | 43 | Helen Keller |
| 17 | Roméo Dallaire | | 44 | Nkebe Kelmandi |
| 18 | Emily Dickinson | | 45 | Robert Kennedy |
| 19 | Frederick Douglass | | 46 | Inayat Khan |
| 20 | Wayne Dyer | | 47 | Ali Khashan |
| 21 | Meister Eckhart | | 48 | Martin Luther King, Jr. |
| 22 | Albert Einstein | | 49 | Jiddu Krishnamurti |
| 23 | Jan Eliasson | | 50 | Dalai Lama |
| 24 | Ralph Waldo Emerson | | 51 | Abraham Lincoln |
| 25 | Pope Francis | | 52 | Archie Mackenzie |
| 26 | Erich Fromm | | 53 | Nelson Mandela |
| 27 | Mohandas Gandhi | | 54 | Horace Mann |
| 28 | Bill Gates | | 55 | Abraham Maslow |

| 56 | Dennis McNamara | 83 | Nikola Tesla |
|----|-----------------|-----|-------------|
| 57 | Rigoberta Menchu | 84 | Mother Theresa |
| 58 | Robert Muller | 85 | Henry David Thoreau |
| 59 | Anaïs Nin | 86 | Paul Tillich |
| 60 | Henri J.M. Nouwen | 87 | Eckhart Tolle |
| 61 | John Pace | 88 | Leo Tolstoy |
| 62 | Rosa Parks | 89 | Desmond Tutu |
| 63 | Plato | 90 | Lau Tzu |
| 64 | Mitri Raheb | 91 | Brian Urquhart |
| 65 | Rainer Maria Rilke | 92 | Sergio Vieira de Mello |
| 66 | Zia Rizvi | 93 | Leonardo Da Vinci |
| 67 | Anthony Robbins | 94 | Swami Vivekananda |
| 68 | Eleanor Roosevelt | 95 | Alice Walker |
| 69 | Theodore Roosevelt | 96 | William Wilberforce |
| 70 | Jalaluddin Rumi | 97 | Paramahansa Yogananda |
| 71 | Bertrand Russell | 98 | Mohammad Yunus |
| 72 | Arthur Schopenhauer | 99 | Zeid  Bin Ra'ad |
| 73 | Albert Schweitzer | 100 | Angel Zuleta |
| 74 | Amartya Sen | 101 | Neill Wright |
| 75 | George Bernard Shaw | | |
| 76 | Catherine of Siena | | |
| 77 | Socrates | | |
| 78 | Edith Södergran | | |
| 79 | Aleksandr Solzhenitsyn | | |
| 80 | George  Soros | | |
| 81 | Harriet Beecher Stowe | | |
| 82 | Rabindranath Tagore | | |

# Acknowledgements

Exactly one year ago, I wrote the first line of this book. I am filled with gratitude to family, friends and colleagues around the globe, who infused and replenished daily excitement for the book over the past twelve months.

I am indebted to Dr. Mitri Raheb who, after reading a first draft, believed in its message and agreed to publish it. Thanks to his trust, I was able to write what was true to my own voice. I also owe my profound thanks to Dr. Ali Khashan for his limitless vision and never ending support in making this book a reality.

I am deeply grateful to Nasser Al-Faqih and Sebastien Gouraud, my constant professional companions and spiritual brothers, whose positive energy, enthusiasm and insightful advice spurred me to continue. I am filled with profound thanks for Sami Abdelshafi, a dear friend, whom I greatly admire and whose interest in this book is particularly important to me. I am also grateful to Omar Bakhet, whose impact and inspiration, largely manifested in this book, spans more than twenty-five years.

My wholehearted appreciation goes to John Pace and Pauline Callaghan, who stood by my side to see this project through, and their son, Patrick Callaghan-Pace, who patiently offered many innovative ideas. Very special thanks to Thomas Dallal for contributing with his professional photographs and artistic advice.

My sincere thanks to Sara Makari, Engred Khoury and Hiba Nasser Atrash at Diyar Publishing, who patiently worked on the text and lay-out, and to Raoul Rajasingham for contributing with creative solutions to the cover. I would also like to express appreciation to Amira Rajasingham for in-depth review of the manuscript, and to Joseph Aguettant, Jennifer Klot, Saudamini Siegrist and Maarten Barends for valuable comments in its final stages.

My very sincere thanks go to Sven and Marie Hessle, who read and commented on the manuscript, and whose gracious and unbending support goes back thirty-five years, well beyond this book. Special thanks to Chris Gunness, who passionately believed in this project, and who introduced me to Kate Hoyland, to whom I owe big thanks for editing the first two chapters and setting the tone for the remainder.

I can hardly find the right words for thanking my family, Ramesh, Amira and Raoul, who stood with me on every step of this journey, and helped to shape the person I am today. My gratitude to you is woven into every page of this book, and I thank you with all my heart.

Finally, I would like to thank my mother, Solbritt, who encouraged and enlightened me till her hands could no longer grip, her legs could no longer carry her, and until she took her last breath on 20 July 2014. Thank you for being my mother.

# *About the Author*

Yasmine Sherif was born in Stockholm in 1964 to a Swedish mother and Egyptian father. She graduated from Stockholm University in 1987 with a Master of Law degree and specialized in international humanitarian law and international human rights law. She has served with the United Nations in Afghanistan, Cambodia, the Balkans, Sudan, and the Middle East, as well as at the United Nations Headquarters in New York and Geneva. Working for the United Nations High Commissioner for Refugees (UNHCR), she initiated and led the first repatriation of refugees to Bosnia following the Dayton Peace agreement in 1995. While with the United Nations Office for the Coordination of Humanitarian Affairs (OCHA) in New York, she oversaw coordination of the Protection of Civilians' agenda in the late 1990s. At the United Nations Development Programme (UNDP), she founded and led the United Nations' largest Rule of Law Assistance Programme, coordinating Rule of Law Assistance to over thirty crisis countries, and served as the Deputy Special Representative of the Programme of Assistance to the Palestinian people. She has been an adjunct Professor at Long Island University (LIU) lecturing on international law and international politics and is the co-founder of the Global Center for Justice & Humanity, and the Director of Diakonia's International Humanitarian Law & Resource Center.

# The Global Center
# for Justice & Humanity

The Global Center for Justice & Humanity is based at Dar Al-Kalima University College in Bethlehem. It is co-founded by Dr. Mitri Raheb, President of the Diyar Consortium, and Dr. Ali Khashan, former Minister of Justice of the Palestinian Authority and founder of the Al-Quds Law School, and Yasmine Sherif. With an integrated vision for the twenty-first century, the Global Center inspires a new approach that recognizes the interdependence between the law, ethics, spirituality, universal values and political commitment in achieving respect for international law and the rule of law based on justice and humanity.

# *Endnotes*

1. First Plenary Meeting of the United Nations General Assembly, Thursday 10 January 1946 at 4 p.m.

2. George Bernard Shaw: The Private Life of George Bernard Shaw: Shaw in love, by Elizabeth Sharland, iUniverse Books, 2000.

3. Confucius: Theories of Democracies, by Terchek and Conte, page 110, Roman & Littlefield, 2001

4. Immanuel Kant: A quest for prayer in a senseless time, Daniel D. Dancer, Trafford Publishing, 2006

5. Plato on Democracy, page 95, Thanassis Samaras, P. Lang 2002.

6. The Kennedy: Dynasty and Disaster, page 621, John H. Davies, S.P.I. Books (Shapolsky Publishers, Inc), 1984.

7. Hammarskjold: A Life, pages 88-89. Roger Lipsey, the University of Michigan Press 2013.

8. 101 Selected Sayings of Mahatma Gandhi, page 19, Irfan Alli, eBookIt.com, 2013.

9. The Little Red Book of Yoga Wisdom, Kelsie Besaw, Skyhorse Publishing, 2014.

10. The Social and Political Thought of Bertrand Russell, page 174, Philip Ironside, Cambridge University Press, 1996.

11. Freedom from the Known (1975 edition) http://www.jkrishnamurti.org/krishnamurti-teachings/view-text.php?tid=48&chid=56784

12. "Second Public Talk at Ojai (21 May 1944) *J.Krishnamurti Online*, JKO Serial No. 440521, *Authentic Report of Ten Talks, Ojai*, 1944 (1945), p. 7, OCLC 67727800.

13. Inspirational Quotes for All Occasions, Chapter 117, Bangambiki Habyarimana, Create Space Independent Publishing Platform, 2013.

14. Mackenzie, Archie, Faith in Diplomacy, A Memoir, page 204, Caux Book, Grosvenor Books, 2002.

15. Interview in the UNESCO Courier, published 27 November, 2010, *Simerg* Homepage.

16. Interview in the UNESCO Courier, published 27 November, 2010, *Simerg* Homepage.

17. Anna Eleanor Roosevelt: the Evolution of a Reformer, Page 140, James R. Kearney, Houghton Mifflin, 1968.

18. Free and Equal: The Universal Declaration of Human Rights at 50, page 11, Mark Smith, Diane Publishing, 1998.

19. *Natural law* assumes that rights are inherent in human nature, while *positive law* refers to that which has been promulgated as law.

20. The Art of Leadership: 500 quotes on how to lead others, Page 17, Eric Garner, Eric Garner & Ventus Publishing, ApS, Bookbone.com, 2012.

21. Interview with General Romeo Dallaire, PBS Frontline, posted 1 April, 2004.

22. Shake Hands with the Devil: Humanity's Failure in Rwanda, page 517, Romeo Dallaire, Random House of Canada, 2009.

23. Roméo Dallaire at USC, Syuzanna Petrosyan, January 25, 2014.

24. William Wilberforce's 1789 Abolition Speech.

25. The 50 most influential people in history, page 162, Michael Wenkart, BoD, Books on Demand, 2014.

26. From Slavery to Citizenship, page 164, Richard Ennals, John Wiley & Sons, 2007.

27. Hope: How Triumphant Leaders Create the Future, page 87, Andrew Razeghi, John Willey & Sons, 2006.

28. Critical Essays on Vaclav Havel, page 93, Marketa Goetz-Stankiewicz, Phyllis Carey, G.K. Hall, 1999.

29. Political Action in Vaclav Havel's Thought: The Responsibility of Resistance, Delia Popescu, Lexington Books, 2012.

30. The Art of Loving: The Centennial Edition, Erich Fromm, A&C Black, 2000.

31. Essays on John Maynard Keynes, psge 268, Milo Keynes, Cambridge University Press, 1980.

32. World Institute for Development Economics Research of the United Nations.

33. Edmund Burke, page 203, Peter James Stanlis, Transaction Publishers, 1967.

34. Quantum Shift in the Global Brain: How the New Scientific Reality Can Change Us and Our World, Ervin Laszlo, Inner Traditions/Bear & Co, 2008.

35. Becoming World Wise: A Guide to Global Learning, page 37, Richard Slimbach, Stylus Publishing, LLC, 2012.

36. Hammarskjold: A Life, page 249, Roger Lipsey, University of Michigan Press, 2013.

37. Inspirational Presence: The Art of Transformational Leadership, page iv, Jeff Evans, Worldclay 2009.

38. Why We War: The Human Investment in Slaughter and the Possibility of Peace, page 418, Al Smith, Lulu.com.

39. A New Earth, Awakening to your life's purpose, page 12, Eckhart Tolle, Penguin Books, 2005.

40. Keys to Educational Psychology, page 405, By Liesel Ebersöhn, Irma Eloff, Juta and Company Ltd, 2004.

41. J. Krishnamurti, Ojaj 1st Public Talk, 3 April 1976, Total Freedom, Krishnamurti Online.

42. Tolstoy's Pacifism, page 144, Colm McKeogh, Cambria Press, 2009.

43. The whole works of Edward Reynolds, Now First Collected, Edward Reynolds, page 89. John Rogers Pitman, 1826.

44. Inspiring Leadership: Leadership Lessons from my Life, page 174, Jonathan Perks, Fisher King Publishing, 2010.

45. An Introduction to the Study of Education, page 60, David Matheson, Routledge, 2014.

46. Critical Thinking Unleashed, page 100, Elliot D. Cohen, Rowman & Littlefield, 2009

47. Poetic Precepts: First Fruits, page Jerrod Biglow, Xlibris Corporation, 2011.

48. Understanding and Interpreting Educational Research, page 19, Ronald C. Martella, J. Ron Nelson, Robert L. Morgan, Nancy E. Marchand-Martella, Guilford Press, 2013.

49. Speaking Professionally: Influence, Power, and Responsibility at the Podium, page 225, Alan Jay Zaremba, M.E. Sharpe, 2011.

50. Peace and Prosperity in an Age of Incivility, page 15, William Eric Davis, University Press of America, 2006.

51. The Philosophy of Spinoza - Special Edition: On God, on Man, and on Man's Well Being, page 250, Baruch Spinoza, Benedictus de Spinoza Special Edition Books, 2010.

52. Swimming in Cosmic Soup, page 67, Russ Otter, Universe, 2013.

53. Opening speech by Zeid Ra'ad Al Hussein United Nations High Commissioner for Human to the High Level Segment of the Human Rights Council, 2 March , 2015.

54. Opening Statement by Zeid Ra'ad Al Hussein United Nations High Commissioner for Human Rights at the Human Rights Council 27th Session, 14 September 2014.

55. The Definitive Executive Assistant and Managerial Handbook: A Professional Guide to Leadership for all PAs, Senior Secretaries, Office Managers and Executive Assistants, page 12, Sue France, Kogan Page Publishers, 2012.

56. Bill Gates on Twitter: post from @gatesfoundation for #Teacher Appreciation Week, 6 May, 2011.

57. Gandhi the Man: The Story of Transformation, Page 30, Eknath Easwaran, The Blue Mountain Center of Meditation, 1997.

58. Parisian Questions and Prologues, Meister Eckhart, Pontifical Institute of Mediaeval Studies, 1974.

59. Political Ethics and The United Nations: Dag Hammarskjöld as Secretary-General, page 173, Manuel Froehlich, Routledge, Oct 29, 2007.

60. Ibid, page 68.

61. To Speak for the World, Speeches and Statements by Dag Hammarskjold, Secretary-General of the United Nations 1953 – 1961, The International Public Servant, Statement to the Press on arrival at

New York International Airport, 9 April 1953, page 63, Kai Falkman, Atlantis, 2005.

62. Hammarskjold: The Political Man, page 55, Dag Hammarskjold, Emery Kelèn, Funk & Wagnalls, 1968.

63. The Laws of Life, Page 663, James Shane, Xulon Press, 2002.

64. The Sayings of Lao Tzu, page 24, Lao Tzu, Lionel Giles, Wilder Publications,2008.

65. The Spiritual Philosophy of the Tao Te Ching,, page 88, Joseph A. Magno, Pendragon Publishing, 2005.

66. What Leaders Do: A Leadership Primer, page 47, Dave Browning, iUniverse, 2009.

67. Interview in the UNESCO Courier, published 27 November, 2010, Simerg Homepage.

68. Setting the Stage for Sustainability: A Citizen's Handbook, Chris Maser, Charles R. Beaton, Kevin M. Smith, CRC Press, 1998.

69. Wit and Wisdom of Gandhi, Nehru, Tagore, Mahatma Gandhi, Jawaharlal Nehru, Rabindranath Tagore, New Book Society of India, 1968.

70. Living at the Source, Yoga Teachings of Vivekananda, page 53, edited by Ann Myren & Dorothy Madison, Shambala, 1993.

71. Ibid.

72. Disturbing Times: The State of the Planet and Its Possible Future, Page 173, Scott T. Firsing, 30° South Publishers, 2008. Note that the original words by Burke referred to "men," while Vieira de Mello's speech before the Security Council referred to "individuals."

73. The Power of Memory in Democratic Politics, page 22, P. J. Brendese, Boydell & Brewer, 2014.

74. Civilization's Quotations: Life's Ideal, page 173, Richard Alan Krieger, Algora Publishing, 2002.

75. Connect the Dots...to Become an Impact Player, page 125, Dick Lynch, iUniverse, Oct 1, 2003.

76. UN News Centre, Interview with Deputy Secretary-General, Jan Eliasson, 27 August, 2012.

77. All Is Mind, page 42, Vir Singh, PartridgeIndia, 2014.

78. Lives That Made a Difference, page 215, P J Clarke, Strategic Book Publishing, 2012.

79. Unleashing the Superhero in Us All, page 60, T. James Musler, Lulu.com, 2008.

80. Long Walk to Freedom: The Autobiography of Nelson Mandela, pages 405-406, Nelson Mandela, Little Brown, 2008.

81. http://en.wikipedia.org/wiki/George_Soros

82. Martin Luther King Jr., Rediscovering Lost Values, Vol 2, page 255, (1992).

83. The Cambridge Companion to Kant, page 1, Paul Guyer, Cambridge University Press, 1992.

84. Time for Outrage: Indignez-Vous, Stephane Hessel, Montpellier, 2010.

85. Paolo Coelho, Twitter, 8 November 2014.

86. Great Speeches by Frederick Douglass, page 134, Frederick Douglass, Courier Corporation, 2013.

87. In the humanitarian world, 'neutrality' means not to take sides with the parties to the conflict, so to gain access to deliver humanitarian assistance. It does not mean not to side with the innocent victims of the conflict, for it is precisely the objective of humanitarian imperative: to side with the victims and attend to their needs and rights. All humanitarian man-made disasters, however, require a political solution that cannot afford to be neutral in the face of the rightful demands of justice, freedom and peace.

88. Living Like Benjamin: Making Dreams Come True, page 92, Capt Brad Borden Usa (Ret ), AuthorHouse, 2007.

89. About Education, Harriet Beecher Stowe Quotes, 1811-1896, Jon Johnson Lewis, Women's History Expert, http://womenshistory.about.com/od/quotes/a/h_b_stowe.htm

90. Key Note, Tavis Smiley, MLK Visiting Professors and Scholars Programme, 28th Annual Martin Luther King Jr. Breakfast Celebration, 2002.

91. Renew America, Don't Let the Lie Come Through You: Never Compromise with Evil, Linda Kimball, 2012, http://www.renewamerica. com/columns/kimball/121106.

92. Quotes by Camus Albert, QuotationsBook.com, page 13.

93. 101 Selected Sayings of Mahatma Gandhi, page 4, Irfan Alli, eBook-It.com, 2013.

94. Inspiring Thoughts Of Mahatma Gandhi, page 1911, Anil Dutt Misra, Concept Publishing Company, 2008.

95. Burke, Select Works, Volume 1, page 196, Edmund Burke, The Lawbook Exchange, Ltd., 2005.

96. The Development of Personality, page 40, C.G. Jung, Routledge, 2014.

97. With Liberty and Justice, page 6, Lynn Robert Buzzard, Victor Books, 1984.

98. The Papers of Martin Luther King, Jr: Rediscovering precious values, page 251, July 1951-November 1955, Martin Luther King (Jr.), Clayborne Carson, Ralph Luker, Penny A. Russell, University of California Press, 1992.

99. Story of Philosophy, page 98, Will Durant, Simon & Schuster, 2012.

100. Gandhian Way: Peace, Non-violence, and Empowerment, page 165, Anand Sharma, Academic Foundation, 2007.

101. Every Day Quote, page 92, Nathalie Montreuil, Lulu.com, 2008.

102. Speech at the celebration of the 180th anniversary of the Virginia Declaration of Rights (16 May 1956).

103. Unpopular Essays, page 106, Bertrand Russell, Routledge, 2009.

104. Life Lessons of Wisdom & Motivation - Volume II: Insightful, Enlightened and Inspirational quotations and proverbs, page 28, M.I. Seka, Providential Press, 2014.

105. One Infinity; a Visible Universe of Invisible Energy: A Shift in Human Consciousness & Evolution of One Love, page 286, Lynda J. Spini, iUniverse, 2009.

106. Quotes by Gandhi Mahatma, page 16, QuotationsBook.com.

107. Searching for Inspiration, page 259, Joseph D. Putti, Trafford Publishing, 2013.

108. Ripples of Hope: Great American Civil Rights Speeches, page 289, Josh Gottheimer, Bill Clinton, Etc, Mary Frances Berry, Basic Books, 2004.

109. elling It Like It Is, page 574, Paul Bowden, Paul Bowden, 2011.

110. The Alchemist, page 141, Paolo Coelho, Editora Rocco, Ltd, 1988.

111. To Seek a Newer World, Robert F. Kennedy, Doubleday, 1967

112. Robert F. Kennedy, University of Cape Town, South Africa, N.U.S.A.S. "Day of Affirmation" Speech June 6th, 1966.

113. The Struggle is My Life, page 259, Popular Prakashan, 1990.

114. Women of Courage: Inspiring Stories of Courage by the Women Who Lived Them, page ix, Katherine Martin, New York Library, 2010.

115. Teachers of Wisdom, page 137, Igor Kononenko, Dorrance Publishing, 2010.

116. Simply Sacred, page 24, Fern Feto Spring, Jennifer Zurick, Lulu.com

117. Transforming Philosophy and Religion, Page 168, Norman Wirzba, Bruce Ellis Benson, Indiana University Press, 2008

118. Desmond Tutu, Interview, Psychology Today, 2005 March/April.

119. Soros on Soros: Staying Ahead of the Curve, page 11, George Soros, Byron Wien, Krisztina Koenen, John Wiley & Sons, 1995.

120. The Guardian, March 2008.

121. Hammarskjold: A Life, page 249, Roger Lipsey, University of Michigan Press, 2013.

122. Frederick Douglass: A Precursor of Liberation Theology, page 38, Reginald F. Davis, Mercer University Press, 2005.

123. The Book of Positive Quotations, page 525, John Cook, Steve Deger and Leslie Ann Gibson, 2007.

124. Simone de Beauvoir, All Said and Done, 1972. http://en.wikiquote.org/wiki/Simone_de_Beauvoir

125. Simone de Beauvoir, The Blood of Others [Le sang des autres], 1946. http://en.wikiquote.org/wiki/Simone_de_Beauvoir

126. http://rosaparksfacts.com/rosa-parks-quotes/

127. If You Ask Me, page 112, Eleanor Roosevelt, Appleton-Century, 1946.

128. Political Ethics and the United Nations: Dag Hammarskjold as Secretary-General, page 49, Routledge, 2007.

129. Markings, Dag Hammarskjold, page 71, translated by Leif Sjöberg and W.H. Auden, Alfred A. Knopf, Inc, 1964.

130. 101 Selected Sayings of Mahatma Gandhi, page 45, Irfan Alli, eBookIt.com, 2013.

131. Teachers of Wisdom, page 14, Igor Kononenko, Dorrance Publishing, 2010.

132. http://www.spaceandmotion.com/Philosophy-Carl-Jung.htm

133. The Anatomy of Judgement, page 50, Philip J. Regal, U of Minnesota Press, 1990.

134. Romeo Dallaire: The Man Who Tried to Stop Rwanda's Slaughter, The General and the Genocide, Terry J. Allen, Amnesty International Magazine.

135. EurActive.com, 4 February, 2015, http://www.euractiv.com/sections/development-policy/uns-eliasson-there-no-peace-without-development-311815

136. Rationality and Freedom, page 51, Amartya Sen, Harvard University Press, 2004.

137. Einstein's Business: Engaging Soul, Imagination, and Excellence in the Workplace, Page 144, Dawson Church, Courtney Arnold, Jeanne House, Elite Books, 2007.

138. Parallel Mind, the Art of Creativity, page 40, Aliyah Marr, Aliyah Marr 2008.

139. Dare to Imagine, page 74, Blake Sinclair, Author House, 2014.

140. Gardner's Art through Ages, Page 701, Helen Gardner, Horst De la Croix, Richard G. Tansey, Harcourt Brace Jovanovich, 1980.

141. Aleksandr Solzhenitsyn: The Ascent from Ideology, page 50, Daniel J. Mahoney, Rowman & Littlefield Publishers, Jan 1, 2001.

142. Executive EQ: Emotional Intelligence in Leadership and Organizations, page 3, Robert K. Cooper, Ayman Sawaf, Penguin, 1998.

143. Beethoven and the Spiritual Path, pp 13-14, David Tame, Theosophical Publishing House, 1994.

144. Naturalopy: The Complete Reference: Naturalopy, page 310, Trung Nguyen, EnCognitive.com, , 2015.

145. http://www.scribd.com/doc/136545662/400-Rumi-Short-Poems-English#scribd

146. Working with Emotional Intelligence, page 333, Daniel Goleman, Bantan Books 1998.

147. Beyond the Conscious Mind: Unlocking the Secrets of the Self, Page 244, Thomas R. Blakeslee, Springer, Nov 11, 2013.

148. Winning the Human Race, page 185, The Independent Commission for Humanitarian Issues.

149. Winning the Human Race, page 185, The Independent Commission for Humanitarian Issues.

150. The World I Live In and Optimism: A Collection of Essays, page 41, Helen Keller, Courier Corporation, 2012.

151. The Power of Intention, page 193, Dr. Wayne Dyer, Hay House, 2010.

152. Reverence for Life Revisited: Albert Schweitzer's Relevance Today, page 115, edited by David Ives, David A. Valone, Cambridge Scholars Publishing, 2009.

153. Gandhi in India, in his own words, page 268, published for Tufts University by University Press of New England, 1987.

154. Ralph Waldo Emerson, page 189, Oliver Wendell Holmes, Reprint Services Corporation, 2007.

155. Time, Conflict, and Human Values, page 22, Julius Thomas Fraser, University of Illinois Press, 1999.

156. From the Unconscious to the Conscious, page 41, Gustave Gelay, William Collins Son, 1920.

157. To Speak for The World, Speeches and Statements by Dag Hammarskjold, Secretary-General of the United Nations 1953 – 1961, Page 213, Kai Falkman, Atlantis AB, 2005.

158. Modern Esoteric: Beyond Our Senses, page 411, Brad Olsen, CCC Publishing, 2014.

159. The World I Live in, page 31, Helen Keller, Wildside Press LLC, 2009.

160. The Idea of Justice, page 130, Amartya Sen, Harvard Press, 2009.

161. Betty Teslenko, A Global Affair, An Inside Look at the United Nations, The UN Spirit by Michael Ryan, page 2104, Jones & Janello, 1995.

162. Treasury Of Spiritual Wisdom A Collection Of 10,000 Powerful Quotations For Transforming Your Life, page 458, Andy Zubko, Motilal Banarsidass Publ., 2003.

163. The Wisdom of Life, page 21, Arthur Schopenhauer, Courier Corporation, 2012.

164. Twitter, Deepak Chopra, 6 August, 2014.

165. To Speak for the World, Speeches and Statements by Dag Hammarskjold, Secretary-General of the United Nations 1953 – 1961, page 204, Kai Falkman, Atlantis, 2005.

166. not just The Small Book of Meditation, page 22, Poonam Dahandania, Veritas / Ravenswood Publishing, 2014.

167. Markings, page 8, Dag Hammarskjold, translated by Leif Sjöberg and W.H. Auden, Alfred A. Knopf, Inc, 1964.

168. Markings, page 29, Dag Hammarskjold, translated by Leif Sjöberg and W.H. Auden, Alfred A. Knopf, Inc, 1964.

169. Nelson Mandela: It Always Seems Impossible Until It's Done, Frances Ridley, ReadZone Books, 2014.

170. Forbes, 12 June, 2013, http://www.forbes.com/sites/mfonobongnsehe/2013/12/06/20-inspirational-quotes-from-nelson-mandela/

171. bid.

172. Markings, page 3, Dag Hammarskjold, translated by Leif Sjöberg and W.H. Auden, Alfred A. Knopf, Inc, 1964

173. A Life in War and Peace, Conversation with Sir Brian Urquhart, 19 March, 1996, Harry Kreisler.

174. Learn by Living, page 168, Eleanor Roosevelt, Westminster John Knox Press, 1960.

175. A Planet of Hope, page 115, Robert Muller, Amity House, Jan 1, 1986.

176. A good man in Rwanda, Marc Doyle, BBC News, 3 April 2014.

177. A good man in Rwanda, Marc Doyle, BBC News, 3 April 2014.

178. Winning the Human Race, page 185, The Independent Commission for Humanitarian Issues, Zed Books, 1988.

179. Follow Your Dreams, page 134, Melanie Young, Lulu.com, 2013.

180. Problem Solving, page 63, Ferguson Publishing, Infobase Publishing, 2009.

181. The Story of My Life: The Autobiography of Helen Keller (Annotated), Chapter IV, Helen Keller, Bronson Tweed Publishing, (originally published 1903).

182. http://www.wisdomquotes.com/quote/helen-keller-20.html

183. — They Fight Like Soldiers, They Die Like Children: The Global Quest to Eradicate the Use of Child Soldiers, Roméo Dallaire, Random House of Canada, 2011. http://www.goodreads.com/quotes/690541-i-think-that-one-of-the-benefits-of-optimism-and

184. Great Thoughts from Masterminds, page 7, A.W. Hall, 1907.

185. http://www.mitriraheb.org/index.php?option=com_content&view=article&id=523&Itemid=95

186. Complete Poems, page 33, Edith Södergran, Bloodaxe Books, 1984.

187. A Few Thoughts for a Young Man: A Lecture, Delivered Before the Boston Mercantile Library Association, on Its 29th Anniversary, page 73, Horace Mann, Ticknor, Reed and Fields, 1850.

188. http://riverbankoftruth.com/2013/04/14/harmony-by-hazrat-inayat-khan/

189. The Wireless Tesla, page 25, Wilder Publications, 2007.

190. Steve Jobs, page 329, Walter Isaacson, Simon & Schuster, 2013.

191. Bulletin of the Atomic Scientists Mar 1979, page 5.

192. Progressive Handbook, http://www.progressiveshandbook. com/handbook/index.php?name=News&file=article&sid=3&the me=Printe

193. Human Nature and Social Theory, Erich Fromm, Cuernavaca (Mexico), 10th March, 1969.

194. Letter from a Birmingham Jail, Martin Luther King Jr., 16 April, 1963.

195. The Return of Merlin, page ix, Deepak Chopra, Wheeler Pub, 1996.

196. The Stranger – Albert Camus, page 107, edited by Harold Bloom, Infobase Publishing, 2009.

197. Future Leaders for The World, Stefano D'Anna, http://www.future-leadersfortheworld.com/2011/814/

198. Interview with David Cooperrider by David Creelman, July, 2001 for the HR.com.

199. Live Life from the Heart, page 107, Mark Black, Strategic Book Publishing, 2011.

200. Interview with Mitri Raheb, on his role as a Social Entrepreneur & Innovator, Bethlehem, December, 2011.

201. Awaken the Giant Within, Tony Robbins, Simon & Schuster, 2012. https://books.google.co.il/books?id=iPpyLpXoY1sC&dq=Robbins+T he+only+limit+to+your+impact+is+your+imagination+and+commit ment&source=gbs_navlinks_s

202. Ibid.

203. Civilization's Quotations: Life's Ideal, page 13, Richard Alan Krieger, Algora Publishing.

204. Elements of Leaders of Character, page 230, Wayne Hogue, WestBow Press, 2013.

205. Tagore Lessons for Living Awake, 8 January, 2015, Jone Bosworth, http://www.incourageleading.com/tagore-lessons-for-living-awake/

206. Leading from the Heart: Sufi Principles at Work, Moid Siddiqui, SAGE Publications India, 2014.

207. Inspiring Creativity: An Anthology of Powerful Insights and Practical Ideas to Guide You to Successful Creating, page 142, Rick Benzel, Creativity Coaching Assoc. Press, 2005.

208. The Big Picture: Life, Meaning, & Human Potential, page 11, Rick C. Mason Ph. D., Rick C. Mason, Rick Mason, J2012.

209. Civilization's Quotations: Life's Ideal, page 29, Ibid.

210. C.G. Jung Foundation on Twitter, 26 March, 2014.

211. Yoga Journal, December 2002 (Letter to a Young Poet, New World Library, 1992).

212. Escape from Freedom, Erich Fromm, page 184, Erich Fromm, 1941.

213. One Home, One Family, One Future, 218, Bashir A. Zikria, Author-House, 2009.

214. Long Walk to Freedom, page 115, Nelson Mandela, Little Brown & Company, 1995.

215. Rousseau, page 62, Timothy O'Hagan, Routledge, Sep 2, 2003.

216. Philosophical Writings: Immanuel Kant, Page 264, Ernst Behler, Bloomsbury Academic, 1986.

217. Foreword II in Escape from Freedom, Erich Fromm, Avon Books, 1965.

218. Forbes, Volume 149, Issues 5-9, Bertie Charles Forbes, Forbes Incorporated, 1992 (One Day in the Life of Ivan Denisovich: A Novel, Aleksandr Solzhenitsyn).

219. Reality in Management, page 89, Arthur H. Kuriloff, McGraw-Hill, 1966.

220. The Maslow Business Reader, page 185, Abraham H. Maslow, Deborah C. Stephens, John Wiley & Sons, 2000.

221. How Can We Bring About Change, Huffington Post, 3 November, 2012.

222. The Social Business Revolution, Dhaka Tribune, 2 July, 2013.

223. Paul Tillich's Philosophy of Art, page 59, Michael F. Palmer, Walter de Gruyter, 1984.

224. The Gulag Archipelago: 1918-1956, Aleksandr Solzhenitsyn, 1973.

225. Do One Thing: Heroes for a Better World, The Emily Fund for a Better World, Rigoberta Menchu Tum, http://www.doonething.org/heroes/pages-m/menchu-quotes.htm

226. Man for Himself: An Inquiry into the Psychology of Ethics, page 237, Erich Fromm, Routledge, Jul 4, 2013.

227. On Being Human, page 103, Erich Fromm, A&C Black, 1997.

228. Liberty for All?, 1820 – 1860, page 8, Joy Hakim, Oxford University Press, 2002.

229. In Search of Leaders, page 130, Hilarie Owen, Wiley, 2000.

230. Markings, page 26, Dag Hammarskjold, translated by Leif Sjöberg & W.H. Auden, Alfred Knopf, 1964.

231. Just a Minute with Paolo Coelho on Digital Media (Reuters), October 14, 2008 by Paolo Coelho.

232. Thoughts, page 14, Horace Mann, H.B. Fuller, 1867.

233. Life Lessons of Wisdom & Motivation - Volume I: Insightful, Enlightened and Inspirational quotations and proverbs Page 208, M.I. Seka, Providential Press, 2014.

234. Higher Self-Improvement, Rumi Quotes, http://www.higher-self-improvement.com/rumi-quotes.html#.VU3RnywcQ5s

235. Anaïs Nin, Wikiquote, http://en.wikiquote.org/wiki/Ana%C3%AFs_Nin

236. Treasury of Spiritual Wisdom A Collection Of 10,000 Powerful Quotations For Transforming Your Life, page 6, Andy Zubko, Motilal Banarsidass Publ., 2003.

237. Gandhi, the Man, page 8, Eknath Easwaran, Nilgiri Press, 1978.

238. A New Way of Living, page 285, Roy Posner, (not dated/Google Books).

239. The UN Secretary-General and Moral Authority: Ethics and Religion in International Leadership, page 117, Kent J. Kille, Georgetown University Press, 2007.

240. 150 Mother Theresa Quotes with Pictures, http://www.verybest-quotes.com/150-mother-teresa-quotes/

241. Eleanor Roosevelt, "In Our Hands" (1958 speech delivered on the tenth anniversary of the Universal Declaration of Human Rights)

242. Love Echo, Poem, Tag Archives: Lau Tzu, https://loveecho.wordpress.com/tag/lao-tzu/page/3/

243. The Essential Tesla, page 121, Nikola Tesla, Wilder Publications, 2007.

244. The Republic Book/Book IX: On Wrong or Right Government, and the Pleasures of Each (Socrates, Adeimantus) Plato.

245. Quotes Emily Dickinson, http://quotesgem.com/author/emily-dickinson

246. Hua Hu Ching: Teachings of Lao Tzu - Page 96, Laozi, Brian Browne Walker, Clark City Press, 1992.

247. Words to Live By: Short Readings of Daily Wisdom, page 92, Eknath Easwaran, Nilgiri Press, 2010.

248. Mohandas K. Gandhi: Thoughts, Words, Deeds, page 37, Ramnarine Sahadeo, Xlibris Corporation, 2011

249. Alice Walker on "Overcoming Speechlessness: A Poet Encounters the Horror in Rwanda, Eastern Congo and Palestine/Israel", Democracy Now, 13 April, 2010.

250. A New Earth, Awakening to your life's purpose, page 19, Eckhart Tolle, Penguin Books, 2005.

251. A New Humanism for the 21st Century, page 5, Irina Bokova, UNESCO, 2010.

252. Markings, page 4, Dag Hammarskjold, translated by Leif Sjöberg & W.H. Auden, Alfred Knopf, 1964.

253. Ibid, page 8.

254. The Science of Spirituality, page 291, Lee Bladon, Lulu.com, 2007.

255. Ibid, Markings, page .43.

256. Ibid, Markings, page .48.

257. Eleanor Roosevelt's Human Rights Legacy, Free Library, http://www.thefreelibrary.com/Eleanor+Roosevelt's+human+rights+legacy.-a0149500525

258. To Speak for the World, Speeches and Statements by Dag Hammarskjold, Secretary-General of the United Nations 1953-1961, page 206, Selected, edited and introduced by Kai Falkman, Atlantis, 2005.

259. World Politics: Trend and Transformation, 2014 – 2015, page 403, Charles Kegley, Shannon Blanton, Cengage Learning, 2014.

260. What about war ..., page 5, Ilie Al., B. Al. Lazar, Dragomir Cristian, Lulu.com

261. Patriotism, Morality and Peace, page 187, Stephen Nathanson, Rowman & Littlefield, 1993.

262. Selected Letters of Rabindranath Tagore, page 72, Rabindranath Tagore, Krishna Dutta, Andrew Robinson, Cambridge University Press, 1997.

263. Elemental geosystems, page 564, Robert W. Christopherson, Prentice Hall, 2007.

264. Cosmic Connections, page 79, Dr. Cheri St. Arnauld, Balboa Press, 2014.

265. Pale Blue Dot: A Vision of the Human Future in Space, page 53, Carl Sagan, Random House, 1994.

266. Carl Sagan Wikiquote, http://en.wikiquote.org/wiki/Carl_Sagan

267. -Dr. Martin Luther King Jr., "Conquering Self-Centeredness" Sermon on August 11, 1957.

268. First Plenary Meeting of the United Nations General Assembly, Thursday 10 January 1946 at 4 p.m.

269. Vaclav Havel, Speech to Congress, February 21, 1990.

270. The Wall of Light: Nikola Tesla and the Venusian Space Ship, the X-12, page 35, Arthur H. Matthews, Health Research Books, 1973.

271. The Essential Tesla, page 149, Nikola Tesla, Wilder Publications, 2007.

272. Albert Schweitzer: a Vindication, page 85, George Seaver, Beacon Press, 1951.

273. Spiritual Renaissance, page 244, Susan Minnaar, AuthorHouse, 2007.

274. Remarks on the Occasion of World Interfaith Harmony Week: Common Ground for the Common Good, General Assembly of the United Nations, President of the 66th Session, New York, 7 February, 2012.

275. © Yasmine Sherif, 2012.

276. The Quotegarden, http://www.quotegarden.com/rumi.html

277. United Earth - Victor Hugo Quotes, Biography & Chronology, http://www.unitedearth.com.au/hugo.html

Made in the USA
San Bernardino, CA
14 October 2015